THE HYDE PARK MISSION STORY LIVES ON

1839-2014 AND BEYOND

STORIES COLLECTED AND EDITED BY

JOYCE PARKER

HYDE PARK BAPTIST CHURCH WMU

AuthorHouse™ LLC
1663 Liberty Drive
Bloomington, IN 47403
www.authorhouse.com
Phone: 1-800-839-8640

Published by AuthorHouse 07/14/2014

ISBN: 978-1-4969-1245-9 (sc)
978-1-4969-1244-2 (e)

authorHOUSE®

HYDE PARK'S MISSION STORY LIVES ON

WOMEN'S MISSIONARY UNION
FROM ITS BEGINNINGS IN TEXAS
THROUGH THE NATIONAL AUXILIARY
TO THE HYDE PARK BAPTIST CHURCH

1839-2014

HYDE PARK BAPTIST CHURCH
3901 SPEEDWAY
AUSTIN, TEXAS 78751

DR. J. KIE BOWMAN, PASTOR
1997-Present

"Laborers together with God"
I Corinthians 3:9

HYMN OF THE YEAR
"WE'VE A STORY TO TELL TO THE NATIONS"

WMU's GUIDING PRINCIPLES

- To Lead the Church
- To pray for and give to missions
- To learn about missions
- To develop spiritually toward a missions lifestyle
- To participate in the work of the church and the denomination

WMU EMPHASIS FOR 2012-2014
THE STORY LIVES ON

WATCHWORD FOR 2013-2014
"We cannot help speaking about what we have seen and heard"
Acts 4:20

TABLE OF CONTENTS

DEDICATION

This book is dedicated to the Lord Jesus Christ,

to Women's Missionary Union, and to all the Hyde Park'ers

who "Pray, Give, and Go" to answer His call to missions.

Acts 1:8 "...you will be my witnesses in Jerusalem and in all Judea and Samaria, and to

the end of the Earth." ESV

Translated to mean "...Austin, Texas, USA, the whole world."

Joyce Parker Version

INTRODUCTION

This is the 125th birthday of Women's Missionary Union, (WMU). In March 1888, the women doing missions all over the states and territories banded together and organized, in order to make more of an impact on world missions. As you will learn in Lillian Brown's historical document in this book, (complete with references) Texas women had been doing foreign missions for several years previous to 1888, but joined in the bigger organization with the ladies "back East." Hyde Park Baptist Church was begun June 1, 1894, and the women began their mission organization December 1896.

At this writing, March 13, 2014, it was last year that I read the book "The Story Lives On" by Wanda S. Lee, Executive Director of WMU, and "somehow" heard a voice in my head, "Joyce, you can do this." So I began collecting mission stories and gathering some historical stories from my fellow Hyde Park'ers, to honor this calling and hopefully to inform our Staff and members of what's going on at Hyde Park Baptist Church outside the worship center. I pray to God our mission story does live on until Jesus comes again!

I will begin this book with a brief history of Hyde Park Baptist Church.

Austin's total population in 1894 was 18,000. The state capitol building was six years old, and the University of Texas campus was a beehive of activity with 447 students enrolled. The new subdivision in North Austin, known as Hyde Park, was just beginning with only a few houses in the area.

Hyde Park Baptist Church was established June 1, 1894, with twelve people meeting in the Austin Electric Street Railway Pavilion between 39th and 40th on Avenue A. Rev. W.D. Beverly preached to this congregation and at the conclusion of his message asked those interested in beginning a new church to come forward. All twelve, including Rev. Beverly, indicated their desire to found a new church in in the Hyde Park neighborhood. The church was named Hyde Park Baptist Church. Rev. Beverly donated two lots at 39th and Speedway for the location of the first building. The men of the church built the building, which they later sold to the Presbyterian Church for $450.00. This 24' x 30' frame building is now at Avenue B and 40th Street as a part of the Hyde Park Presbyterian Church.

A second sanctuary building was begun in 1911. This building was not completed and dedicated until April 2, 1916, under the leadership of Pastor W. H. Fortney, but services were held in the unfinished sanctuary until that time. An educational building was added in 1939. In 1948-49, under the leadership of Pastor Scott Tatum, another sanctuary, called "Tatum's Folly," was constructed. It was so large they began with theater seating, but they only put seats half-way back. Very soon, with almost explosive membership growth, more seats were added.

Another educational building was added in 1958. Dr. Ralph M. Smith was called as pastor in June 1960, and the church entered a period of sustained growth in attendance. Many more buildings would be built over the next thirty years to accommodate the dynamic growth of Hyde Park. In the early 1980's, the present sanctuary was built, under the leadership of Dr. Ralph M. Smith. It was dedicated in 1984. The architect of this building project, which also added more Sunday School space and more offices, was Mr. Don Tew, one of Hyde Park's "home-grown boys!"

Hyde Park Baptist Church has grown to include the whole block from 39th to 40th streets on Speedway to Avenue F, plus a 4 story parking garage across the street on Speedway and a Christian Life Center on the Northwest corner of 40th and Ave F, and several other properties around the church neighborhood that is used for other church and school activities.

Under the guidance of Mr. Bob Ed Shotwell, the Hyde Park Primary School was begun in 1968, then the high school in 1980.

With the acquisition of the Quarries, a 57-acre quarry, which is now a spring-fed lake, another CLC (Christian Life Center), and sports fields were added to Hyde Park Baptist Church in 2006. The High School was built in 2009, and the students moved there. Now there's the Quarries Church that meets in the school, with Dr. Bowman preaching "on the move" between campuses. I am unaware of plans for the future building projects for the Quarries Church on the Quarries property.

In 1997, Dr. J. Kie Bowman was called as pastor and is still serving at Hyde Park Baptist Church. He has facilitated the use of new technology in this 21st century. Besides radio and TV, he has integrated the Internet and social media to show the world our church services for the furtherance of the Great Commission.

Truly the Lord has used Hyde Park Baptist Church in His great work and has blessed the growth of our church in Austin. We anticipate the present and future blessing of God upon our work.

WMU Mission Groups

ADULTS ON MISSION

WOMEN ON MISSION

ACTEENS

GIRLS IN ACTION

ROYAL AMBASSADORS

MISSION FRIENDS

"My house shall be called a house of prayer for all nations"

Jesus said, "My house shall be called a house of prayer for all nations" and in the book of James it says, "the prayer of a righteous man is powerful and effective."

At Hyde Park Baptist Church we take these verses to heart and strongly believe in the power of prayer! We believe that prayer moves the hand that moves the world. We consider it an honor and privilege to pray for you and your loved ones. You may submit a prayer request online at any time by going to www.hpbc.org/prayer, or by calling our 24-hour prayer phone line and leaving a message. That number is 512-465-8388.

Our prayer ministry is staffed with wonderful volunteer prayer warriors who are called by God and committed to praying for others. Their prayer support is vital to the life of our church! If you would like to be a part of this ministry, please check out the opportunities listed on the website.

HISTORY OF WOMEN'S MISSIONARY UNION IN TEXAS
AND HYDE PARK BAPTIST CHURCH
1839-1994
Written by Dr. J. Lillian (Wheeles) Brown
April 1994
Austin, Texas

The Missions-Minded Women of the Hyde Park Baptist Church, in its Centennial year (1894-1994), follow in the train of determined pioneer women and supportive men.

According to Mrs. B. A. Copass's chapter, "Women and Their Work", in The Centennial Story Of Texas Baptists (1936), the first Women's Society of Texas was organized in the Old North Church of Nacogdoches in 1839. The two brave women who founded this group were Mrs. Massie Millard (remembered for a prayer meeting in a thicket in 1832 while seeking safety from the Indians), and Annette Bledsoe, sister-in-law of Sam Houston.

Annette (because of her connections) was able to do the work of a home missionary for the next twenty-five years, traveling on horseback and by wagon to churches and schools, distributing books and leaflets and urging the women to organize.

She witnessed the formation of Union Association in 1840. Eleven more Associations were formed over the next fifteen years in different parts of the state until on July 24, 1857, The Austin Baptist Association was formed with 13 churches, six of them out of the Colorado Association. Thirty-five years later, the Baptist Church of Elgin was founded (1892), and its pastor would be the visionary who led in starting the Hyde Park Baptist Church (1894).

One of the supportive men in those early days was R. C. Buckner (the beloved founder of Buckner Orphan's Home). He moved from Kentucky to Paris, Texas in 1861. As pastor, he promoted an organization called the Ladies Sewing Circle, which made enough money to help him build a meetinghouse.

The idea spread to Dallas in 1872 where an Industrial Society for Women was formed. It gave $500 of its earnings to lay the foundation of the First Baptist Church.

Opposition to women's societies from leading preachers caused many trials and tears among the women, but they prayed on. Mrs. Elizabeth Pyle, who had been a student in Ladonia Institute and whose father, Rev. Noah Miller, labored in North Texas, wrote of the problem from personal experience. She said, "My father being a minister, I was associated from my earliest recollection with ministers and leading Baptists of those yesterdays. Even the more enlightened of them were shy of women's societies. They were not sure that women knew how to carry on alone, not realizing that their women had wonderful training in managing their homes, their children, and even their husbands, though the poor dears knew it not."

One supportive preacher made a perceptive comment. He said, "The hostility of some men to women's active gospel work looks a little like envy and jealousy rather than stern regard for theories of inspiration and scriptural prohibition."

Two other staunch champions of women's societies were Dr. William Cary Crane, President of Baylor at Independence (1863-1885), and Dr. J. B. Link, editor of the Texas Baptist Herald, which began publishing in1865. Wherever he spoke, Dr. Crane urged the organization of Women For Missions. In fact, the first Texas Home Mission Society was organized at Independence in 1878 with Baylor women as officers: Mrs. Fannie Breedlove Davis, President, and Miss Anne Luther, Secretary.

Dr. Crane, with Dr. H. A. Tupper, Executive Secretary of the Foreign Mission Board of the Southern Baptist Convention, began urging the organization of women in connection with the mission causes of the SBC. The report that these men gave to the Convention in Nashville in 1878 was really the opening of the door for Mission Work among Baptist women of the South.

Word of the favorable response to Crane and Tupper was all those Baylor women needed. Fannie B. Davis and Anne Luther began a laborious letter-writing campaign to representative women across the state.

So, on Sunday afternoon in October 1880, in the basement of the First Baptist Church of Austin (while the men-only State Convention was meeting upstairs), a group of women representing twelve Mission Societies in Texas organized the Women's Missionary Union Of Texas.

Fannie Davis was elected President, and Mrs. O. C. Pope was elected the Corresponding Secretary. At the same time, upstairs, Miss Luther was being examined by the State Board as prospective foreign missionary. Annie was approved and recommended to the Foreign Mission Board, who assigned her to Brazil. Shortly after her appointment, she married W. B. Bagby, and in January of 1881, they sailed for Brazil. (The story of the Bagby's in Brazil is another exciting chapter in the continuing history of Christian missions.)

This newly organized WMU of Texas undertook the support of their first woman foreign missionary by forming 345 Anne Luther Societies. In very hard times, these women raised $50 a month.

It was during Fannie B. Davis' presidency of Texas WMU (1880-1895) that the "long prayed for vision" of an organization for the Baptist women of the South became a reality.

Again, in the basement of another church, Broadway Methodist Church in Richmond, Virginia, on May 14, 1888, (while 835 men convened the SBC at the First Baptist Church), the Woman's Missionary Union Auxiliary To The Southern Baptist Convention was organized.

A memorable statement came from our Texas WMU President during the suspense-filled roll call of state representatives. "Virginia requested leave to retire for consultation. As the roll call was read, 10 states heartily favored organization: Maryland, South Carolina, Missouri, Tennessee, Texas, Arkansas, Florida, Georgia, Louisiana, and Kentucky. Virginia and Mississippi preferred to delay action, and the women from

West Virginia, North Carolina, and Alabama were not delegated representatives." After Texas' WMU Director Fannie Davis' affirmative vote, she added, "This movement is not for 'Women's Rights'; though we have our rights, the highest of which is the right for service!"

No doubt, Mrs. Davis was trying to reassure the brethren by contrasting WMU with the Women's Rights movement begun by the Quakers in 1848, which sponsored the first Woman's Rights Convention in all of history; as well as the National Woman's Suffrage Association, which began in 1869. [It is ironic that the slaves won their freedom and the right to vote (13th and 15th Amendments) before women of the USA were granted the right to vote (19th Amendment) in 1920.]

Tupper had sensed the change in conditions; saw the clubs of a secular nature affording development of women, and he wanted to use the best in devoted womanhood for MISSIONS.

Later, E. Y. Mullins, at the SBC in Nashville, called attention to the convention's gratitude for WMU's auxiliary status (unlike other denominations where women solicited funds and sent our their own missionaries) and begged that more recognition be granted women on boards lest they not always wish to remain auxiliary.

While women were getting organized in Texas (1880) and in the South (1888), new churches and Associations were multiplying. By 1894, Austin had a population of 18,000; The University of Texas had an enrollment of 447; and the Austin Baptist Association had grown to 33 churches with a combined membership of 2,849.

And a famous sculptress from Germany, Elisabet Ney, completed her castle-like studio in the Hyde Park community where she was commissioned to do statues of Stephen F. Austin and General Sam Houston for the Texas Exhibit at the World's Centennial Exposition in Chicago. (Four years after her death in 1907, her studio was turned into a museum and is one of the oldest art museums in Texas, a matter of pride for the residents of Hyde Park.)

In the year 1894, the First Baptist Church of Elgin, Texas, "loaned" its pastor and some former members to help organize the Hyde Park Baptist Church. W. D. Beverly, the Elgin pastor, and his family had come to Texas from South Carolina in 1871 (after the Civil War) to help restore the scattered congregations in East and Central Texas. After pastoring in Elgin (the church founded in 1892), Beverly became aware of the need for a church in the Hyde Park area. He and his son-in-law visited the E. D. Durfees, who had moved to Austin from Elgin, to discuss the possibility of starting a Baptist Church. Mrs. Durfees agreed to canvass the few Baptist families in the area to see if there was interest in organizing a new church. Her response to the preacher's vision and the people's response to her visits accounted for the founding of the Hyde Park Baptist Church.

It is not known how many more were present on that Sunday morning of June 1, 1894 at the Austin Electric Railway Pavilion, but twelve responded to the Rev. Beverly's invitation to organize a new church. The charter members were Rev. and Mrs. W. D. Beverly, Mr. And Mrs. Henry Loveless, Mr. and Mrs. Thomas Dixon, Mr. and Mrs. E. D. Durfee and their daughter, Willie Dewey Durfee, Mrs. Mary Burdett and her son, W. H. Burdett, and Mrs. N.D. Barron; Five men and seven women.

Rev. Beverly was called as pastor, a clerk/treasurer was named, the church was named, and the Sunday School was established the following Sunday.

In two years, late in December of 1896, The Ladies Missionary Society was organized with Mrs. Thomas Dixon as president. They must have started saving their butter and egg money because by 1909 the foundation for the next meetinghouse was laid on property purchased by these women. They would not be the last women to contribute to the property now owned by the church.

During the period between 1910 and 1916, the church was near to losing its property to a Catholic church, which held the mortgage. A widow member of Hyde Park mortgaged her house to avoid foreclosure. Also, a church between Corpus Christi and the Valley heard about the problem and wired money. (Information received from Norman Dingmore, Manager of the Baptist Book Store at Arlington, while at the WMU Leadership Training Conference on August 8, 1989. His mother, Laura Lindsey Dingmore, whose family moved to Hyde Park area in 1907, told him of the unnamed woman's action.)

Corroborating evidence of financial problems was revealed in 1910 Austin Baptist Association Minutes. "The Association assisted Hyde Park and seven other churches in paying the salaries of their pastors."

The meeting house built on the Beverly's lots was sold to the Presbyterians soon after Pastor Beverly's death in 1889, with both churches sharing the building until the Baptists entered an unfinished sanctuary in 1911, situated on the southeast corner of 39th and Speedway. Not until April 2, 1916 was the second sanctuary completed and dedicated under the leadership of Pastor W. H. Fortney.

Mrs. W. H. Dodson's history of the WMU in the Austin Association reveals the continued struggle for credibility with the brethren. "In 1892, on motion of J. M Black, the minutes of the WMU were permitted to be embodied in the minutes of the Association. In 1889, the WMU report was read by Mrs. J. L. Uredenburg, the first time a report was read by a woman." [More lenient than the SBC brethren.]

A SHORT HISTORY OF THE SUNBEAMS

The mission organizations for children and young people in the South eventually became the responsibility of the Women's Societies, and training of leaders became their crucial task.

The Sunbeam Band, whose name was changed to Mission Friends In 1970, began in 1886 before the national Woman's Missionary Union was organized. In fact, this missionary awakening, started by Mary Webb in Boston (1800) spread to Virginia and other Southern states where there are early records of juvenile missionary societies and Children's Cent Societies. The first Sunbeam Band is credited to George Braxton Taylor, "who, as a young pastor, coupled his missionary earnestness with the zest of Mrs. Anna L. Elsom in his church at Fairmont, Va. They started the band to give children missionary intelligence."

" By 1889, a total of 284 Sunbeam Bands reported 8,000 to 10,000 members. Correspondence between Taylor and the Woman's Missionary Union Executive Committee led to a plan of work for 1892 which urged the society in every church to appoint a bright, consecrated woman to organize children's bands, attend meetings and impress upon children the importance of praying for people on mission fields. In 1896, at the Foreign Mission Board's request, Woman's Missionary Union assumed full responsibility for development of the Sunbeams.

Association records go back only to 1920. That year HPBC had a struggling WMU of 15 members and one Sunbeam Band. Mrs. Edgar Olfers was WMS president and Mrs. L. W. Denman the Sunbeam leader.

"In 1955, Elsie Rives, a trained specialist in elementary education, became the first Convention-wide Sunbeam secretary.

Hyde Park is fortunate to have a "bright, consecrated woman," Mrs. Becky Shipp, directing its MISSION FRIENDS in 1994. She, with her volunteers, works with preschool boys and girls, believing that "even infants may gain foundations in missions if cared for in a proper environment."

A SHORT HISTORY OF YWA

The next group to be organized and placed under the leadership of the women was the Young Woman's Auxiliary, for young women ages 16-25. Under the leadership of Fannie S. Heck, who returned to the presidency of the national WMU in 1906, YWA began its organized life in 1907 with the watchword: "They that are wise shall shine like the brightness of the firmament; and they that turn many to righteousness as the stars forever and ever." (Daniel 12:3)

A logo was adopted and in 1912 the song, "O Zion Hast," was selected as YWA's theme.

YWA grew rapidly to 992 organizations in two years. "The model camp for WMU was begun in 1924 for the YWA. It was the dream of Juliette Mather in her second year as WMU's young peoples' secretary. It was the first regularly sponsored South-wide Baptist event at Ridgecrest, North Carolina, and it continued through 1970, when YWA was changed into two new age-level groups.

Hyde Park's first YWA was in 1923. The one that meant the most to this editor was provided in 1938 with encouragement from the pastor and his wife, E. E. and Grace Wheeless. Gussie Mae Morrow was City-wide YWA president in 1939. Miss Juliette Mather invited the pastor's daughter, Lillian, to play piano for the Ridgecrest YWA Retreat in 1940. There she joined more than 1200 young women from over the South for life-changing experiences.

"In addition to YWA in local churches, many were organized on college campuses and in hospitals. The Ann Hasseltine YWA for young college women was organized in 1910, and the Grace McBride YWA for nurses in 1923." Ann Hasseltine was the heroine who went out to India and Burma with her husband, Adoniram Judson, in 1812—to suffer deprivation and death so very much like the Lord Jesus Christ. (Lillian joined the Ann Hasseltine YWA when she entered Baylor in the fall of 1940.) Grace McBride was the heroine for nurses." She was a graduate of the WMU Training School, appointed as a Foreign Mission Board nurse in Hwanghsen, China, in 1916. Two years later, wartime needs caused her to join the Red Cross. She was sent to Siberia where she died of typhus fever in 1918.

Changing times among young women and new organizations for college young people led WMU in 1965 to transfer direction of the college and hospital YWA's to the BAPTIST STUDENT UNION program.

ACTEENS

Teen age-level groups formed out of YWA in 1970 were called ACTEENS and BAPTIST YOUNG WOMEN. "ACTEENS was set up for girls in grades 7 through 12. STUDIACT was written as the individual achievement plan through which the ACTEENS would study and work directly in mission projects. The ACTEEN ACTIVATORS plan was launched with a pilot team of girls in 1976. (ACTIVATORS must complete at least 50 hours of supervised training before going as a group to a designated spot of assistance in missions.) Prior to 1986, all ACTEEN ACTIVATORS worked in the US under commission by the Home Mission Board. The number has grown every year but one. In 1986, 65 teams of 581 persons served. The ten-year total was 170 teams with 2,354 volunteers. ACTEEN ACTIVATORS ABROAD was piloted in 1986 in cooperation with the Foreign Mission Board. Five teams went to Jamaica or the Philippines and 36 persons were involved."

Hyde Park's ACTEENS have been active since 1972. The leader, Jan Sutton, became director in 1985 and her helpers have involved the girls in four foreign mission projects and three home mission projects: Hong Kong, Canada and Germany; San Antonio, Houston, Garfield and California. The Foreign Mission Board has assigned them to Caracas, Venezuela for the summer of 1994.

BAPTIST YOUNG WOMEN

BYW was the other new program growing out of the reorganization of YWA in 1970. BYA was targeted for students, young career women and others. The age range originally was 18-29; effective in 1988, BYW included women ages 18-34.

Though originally planned as a church organization, it was extended to college campuses in 1977. It was then modified to suit campus plan. In 1986, Campus BYW was reported on 81 campuses. Even the US Military Academy at West Point had a BYW.

The first national conference for BYW was held in 1976 in connection with the WMU Annual Meeting.

By 1985 BYW Enterprisers was introduced, similar to the Activator program in Acteens. The first Enterpriser Team of campus BYWs from Oklahoma Baptist University served for a week in inner city New Orleans.

Baptist Young Women in Hyde Park Baptist Church started well when the 1970 change came. But its continuity has suffered. The graying of faithful Baptist Women indicates the importance of giving attention to this "missing link" in the business of Missions Education.

ROYAL AMBASSADORS

In May 1908, in response to the need for an over-all organization to bind together the groups already existing in the churches and to reach more boys, WMU voted to promote the Order Of Royal Ambassadors.

The first chapter organized was the Cary Newton Chapter of Goldsboro, N. C. It was organized by Mrs. W. M. Petway, who was so interested that she left the WMU meeting early and hurried home so that the boys in her church could start this first chapter in the SBC.

In 1943, WMU employed the first full-time secretary, J. Ivyloy Bishop.

G.L. Boles of Lonoke, Arkansas in 1917, after he became the state leader, wrote the initiation service.

The four ranks for boys 9-12 are Page, Squire, Knight, and Ambassador. For boys 13 and up, they may work on two higher ranks: Ambassador Extraordinary and Ambassador Plenipotentiary, whose requirements were chosen from 50 projects representing handicraft, sports, scientific research, missionary facts and biography, Bible knowledge and actual visits to mission fields. The chapters are organized according to age.

Virginia WMU held the first RA Camp in 1917 at Virginia Beach. The first national Royal Ambassador Congress was held in August of 1953 with 5,000 boys present.

Women's Missionary Union recommended in 1939 that Brotherhood Mission Organizations in local churches cooperate more. More became counselors. SBC finally adopted the 1953 WMU proposal to transfer sponsorship of RAs to the Brotherhood Commission.

Though Hyde Park does not have a Brotherhood Mission Organization, the Royal Ambassador Chapter for Boys in grades 1-6 is very active because of leadership of Kyle Thompson; the Children's Minister, Wayne Gerhardt; and the present director, Henry Klingemann.

Editor's Note: (Joyce Parker)

WMU leaders were invited to discuss the possibility of assuming responsibility for missions resources for RA and Challengers…[Below] is the news release from NAMB sharing the great news that, beginning with the 2012–2013 church year, WMU will be home for both organizations of boys. But in Texas, TBM is keeping RA's rather than WMU. They have managed it under the Brotherhood very well.

GIRL'S AUXILIARY

After organization of YWA in 1907, girls over 16 had a definite place in WMU, and Sunbeam bands had been the missionary organizations for children under 12 for several years. In 1908, referring to boys and girls between 12 and 16 as "the missing link," WMU asked that programs be provided for this age group.

Girl's Auxiliary then dates its actual organization to 1913 when Junior Young Woman's Auxiliaries were first listed as a separate organization. Girl's Auxiliary became the official name in 1914.

Mary Faison Dixon, elected Young People's Secretary In 1916, introduced a correspondence course for GA counselors the following year. Volunteer help succeeded her until Juliette Mather became Young People's Secretary in 1921.

"We've a Story to Tell to the Nations" was selected the GA hymn in 1921; "Arise, Shine; For Thy Light is Come" (Isaiah 60:1) was chosen as the watchword; and an initiation service was written.

Forward Steps were introduced in 1928: Maiden, Lady-In-Waiting, Princess, and Queen.

Because of enthusiastic response, two higher steps were added in 1933 for Intermediate GA's: Queen-With-Scepter and Queen Regent.

The Star Ideals—"abiding in Him through prayer, advancing in wisdom by Bible study, acknowledging my stewardship, adorning myself with good works, and accepting the challenge of the Great Commission—" reflected the fundamentals of Woman's Missionary Union.

By 1954, Girl's Auxiliary was the largest evangelical denominational organization in the world. Many missionaries attribute their call to experiences in GA's, especially the summer camps.

The Association Minutes show that the first Girl's Auxiliary in Hyde Park Baptist Church was organized in 1928. Miss Hollie Lindsay was the President of WMU that year. The records reveal that Girl's Auxiliary flourished from then until the 1970 change to Girls In Action, which has continued to grow.

GIRLS IN ACTION

The reorganization within WMU in 1970 changed the name Girl's Auxiliary to Girl's In Action, preserving the popular initials, GA. It is for girls in grades 1 through 6.

The individual achievement plan for Girl's in Action is called Mission Adventures, through six levels of activity. Each girl receives a badge on completion of the projects required in each level.

The 1994 Director in Hyde Park's WMU is Helen Pike, succeeding Judith Koon. Judith became a leader in Girl's in action in July of 1970, in time to be a part of the change to Girl's In Action. She became director in 1972 and served in that office until 1992, twenty years of outstanding leadership.

MEMORABLE WORDS FROM HISTORIANS

REV. J. N. Marshall, an outstanding preacher/evangelist/missionary in the early days of the Austin Baptist Association, gave an historical address at the 1932 Annual Association of ABA (1857-1932).

He presented statistical information from six periods that are significant for showing where Hyde Park entered the picture. This history will excerpt the dated, number of churches, number of Sunday Schools, number of Training Unions, number of WMUs and the total number of members in the churches:

DATE	CH'S	S.S.	T.U.	WMU	MEMBERS
1857	14	1	0	0	513
1894	33	27	0	9	2,849
1907	34	26	0	10	3.117
1912	42	32	0	18	4,587
1922	21	21	14	15	3,268
1931	35	32	15	25	7,850

This chart raises one question: What happened in 1922? It appears that about half of the churches either disbanded or withdrew from the Association.

On Missions, Rev. Marshall said, "This body was organized with the missionary spirit and purpose. It was, in 1857, perhaps the most western Baptist missionary organization in the world."

In the early years, the Association employed one or two missionaries each year at $1.00 per day to ride horseback into unknown areas to preach and organize Baptist churches.

His paragraph on Woman's Missionary Union is a classic: "From that far-away day that a company of devoted women expressed interest in the earthly labors of their Lord and Savior and broke their alabaster boxes of love and devotion at His cross and His empty tomb, down through the labors of the Apostles to the Gentiles helping him as he gratefully acknowledged, down through the Christian centuries have women been first and foremost in the churches giving their allegiance and help to every good cause even to this present day. It is, however, of recent date that women have banded themselves together in organized bodies for definite work. The first resolution calling attention to it in the Southern Baptist Convention was in 1878. Coincidently, the first local organization of women in a church in Texas was at Independence the same year. [He wasn't aware of the 1839 organization in Nacogdoches.] Two years after this, or in 1880, the Baptist State-wide organization of our women was effected. From that date, the women of the association have been a mighty power."

From Baptist Historian, Dr. H. Leon McBeth's article, "Perspectives on Women in Baptist Life," in July, 1987 Journal of the SBC Historical Commission: "The historical records confirm that women have attended our churches, prayed for our ministries, given sacrificially to our causes, taught our Sunday Schools, influenced the content and tone of our worship services, sung in our choirs, cared for our nurseries, led our Vacation Bible Schools, provided and cared for our baptismal robes, divided out the elements for the Lord's Supper, opened their homes for our visiting preachers, and in many cases swept and vacuumed our church buildings. You have fed our preachers; God knows how much fried chicken and coconut pie you have dished up for our pastors and visiting evangelists! And through it all, you have kept a sweet spirit and continued to model in word and deed the very best of the Christian life.

"After the Women's Missionary Union was formed in 1888, the WMU prepared an annual report to the convention. Though women wrote the report, they could not present it; for the first forty years the annual report was read to the convention by a man. When the president of WMU first gave her own report, it proved so controversial that several men walked out rather than witness such desecration. For several years, it was customary for the convention to move from the church sanctuary to the Sunday School assembly rooms when it was time for the WMU report, so that a woman would not stand behind the pulpit.

"No fact of Baptist history is clearer than the fact that women have set the pace for Baptist involvement in missions…What had been 'women's work' now became the task of the entire church.

"I feel very deeply that the time has come for a moratorium on men making authoritative pronouncements about women. You must do your own speaking. You must define your own rules. You must become biblical scholars and interpret for yourselves, and for us, what it means to be a woman; you must research Baptist history and recover your part of the heritage; you must discern how God is dealing with you; and you must determine if God is calling you and if so, to what; and you and only you can determine your proper response to God's call."

REFERENCES

Allen, Catherine B.; *A CENTURY TO CELEBRATEE.HISTORY OF WOMAN'S MISSIONARY UNION. Birmingham; WMU 1987*

AUSTIN BAPTIST ASSOCIATION MINUTES OF ANNUAL MEETING AND CHURCH REPORTS. Austin ABA, 1920-1993

Baker, Robert A. ; *THE BLOOMING DESERT. A Concise History of Texas Baptists. Waco: Word Books, Pub. 1970.*

Brown, J. Lillian. *HYDE PARK BAPTIST CHURCH. 92 YEARS OF MINISTRY. Austin: Desktop Pub., 1986. (Pamphlet done for Church Library Presentation.)*

Copass, Mrs. B.A. "The Women and Their Work," *CENTENNIAL STORY OF TEXAS BAPTISTS. Dallas: Baptist General Convention of Texas, 1936. (202-241)*

Cox, Norman Wade. Ed. *ENCYCLOPEDIA OF SOUTHERN BAPTISTS VOL. 1 (Ab-Ken) Nashville: Broadman Press, 1958*

Elliott, L.R. "Historic Churches I Texas." (621-623)
Weeks, Dorothy Louise, "Girl's Auxiliary." (60-562). *ENCYCLOPEDIA OF SOUTHERN BAPTISTS VOL. II (Ker-Yu) Nashville: Broadman Press, 1958*
Bishop, J. Ivyloy. "Royal Ambassadors." (1174-1175)

Hamric, Ethalee, "Young Woman's Auxiliary". (1551-1552)
Mather, Juliette. "Sunbeam Band" (1314) and
     "Woman's Missionary Union". (1506-1527)

McBeth, H. Leon, "Perspectives on Women in Southern Baptist Life." *BAPTIST HISTORY AND HERITAGE.* VOL XXII, No. 3 Nashville: Historical Commission of SBC. July 1987. (4-10)

Montague, Rodney. Chairman of Homecoming Day. *SIXTY-EIGHT YEARS OF FAITH.* Booklet. Austin: Hyde Park Baptist Church Pub., July 1962

Murray, Lois Smith. *BAYLOR AT INDEPENDENCE.* WACO: Baylor University Press, 1972

Sapp, James M., *A PERSISTENT PEOPLE.* The 125th Anniversary of Austin Baptist Association. Austin: ABA 1982.

Smith, Ralph M. Ed. "The Church Focuses on Its Mission Education Ministry," *THE HYDE PARK BAPTIST.* Vol. 49, February 23, 1994, No. 6.

Staff. "Elisabet Ney: Ushering Texas Into a New Era," *AUSTIN AMERICAN-STATESMAN.* Austin: Cox Publishers, 1994

Tew, Don. *75 YEARS. HYDE PARK BAPTIST CHURCH TOWARD A CENTURY OF SERVICE.* Austin: HPBC, 1969

Wheeless, E.E. Memoirs of Pastorate at Hyde Park, 1938-1942. Manuscript, 1950

This is a certificate indicating that Hyde Park's WMU has completed all the Steps of Achievements required to be recognized by the National WMU. This activity was discontinued shortly after we won this award.

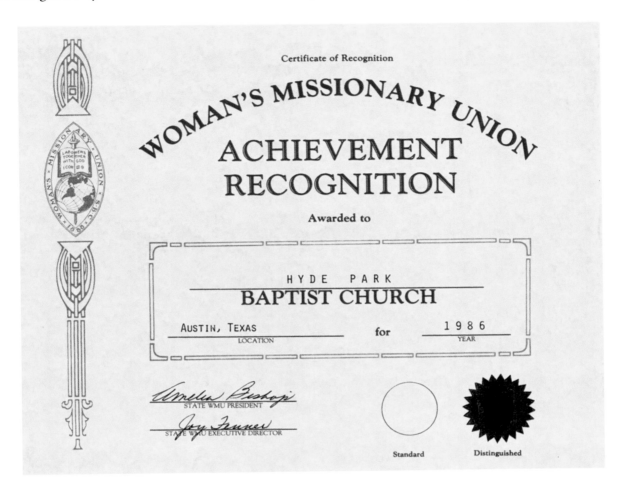

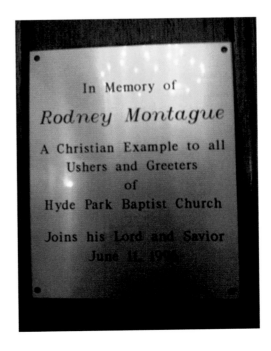

MEMORIALS

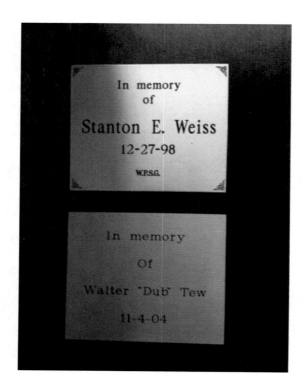

Guidelines of Woman's Missionary Union
Hyde Park Baptist Church

Name: The name of this organization shall be the Woman's Missionary Union of Hyde Park Baptist Church.

Object:

The purpose of this organization shall be to promote and support missions through prayer and giving to missions, to educate in missions by providing mission organizations for women, girls, and preschoolers; engage in mission action reaching beyond the church family and personal witnessing with people who are not Christians and giving them the opportunity to accept Christ as their Savior, and to help the church fulfill its mission.

Membership:

Woman's Missionary Union shall be composed of those enrolled in Adults on Mission, Women on Mission, Acteens, Girls in Action, Royal Ambassadors, and Mission Friends.

Standing Rules:

Ministering to a hospitalized member or at the death of a family member shall be taken care of by the group in which he/she is a member. A suggested limit is $25.

A memorial gift for persons outside of the organization will be limited to $25.

Note: Guidelines were last updated 2005.

Officers

The officers shall be the Director, Secretary/Treasurer, Coordinator of Women on Mission, Director or Leader of each age level organization and the Church wide Missions Coordinator. These officers shall be elected annually in the month of May and submitted to the church for election according to the church program.

All directors, coordinators, leaders, chairmen and officers of WMU shall be active member of the church.

The officers, directors, coordinators, leaders and chairmen shall assume office September 1 and serve until August 31 of the following year. Age level organizations will begin the year according to the church fall program.

The officers, directors, coordinators, leaders and chairmen shall perform the duties set out for them in the current manual and/yearbook of WMU and the Southern Baptist Convention. The officers' duties may be determined by the WMU Director and the leadership team.

Committees:

WMU shall have committees such as, but not limited to, the Nominating, Directory, and Mission House. The duties shall be determined by the current yearbook and outlined by the WMU leadership team.

EDITOR'S NOTE:
Hyde Park Baptist Church no longer has a mission house.

Past Presidents and Directors

Mrs. Thomas Dixon organized the first Missionary Society in 1896.

WMS Presidents
1920-1970

WMU Directors
1971-2013

Mrs. A. McMillan
Mrs. F. R. Barron
Mrs. C. L. Sansing
Mrs. T. J. Ing
Miss Hollie Lindsey
Mrs. Edgar Olfus
Mrs. May Caughey
Mrs. C. E. Watt
Mrs. J. S. Robinson
Mrs. R. C. Hallmark
Mrs. E. E. Wheeless
Mrs. R. K. Wycoff
Mrs. J. F. Cook
Mrs. Ray Bolton
Mrs. Roland Taylor
Mrs. Carter Lester
Mrs. Ed Hornsby
Mrs. W. A. Tew III
Mrs. Albert Miller
Mrs. O. H. Baldwin
Mrs. Pat Parker
Mrs. C. O. Smith
Mrs. W. E. Griffin
Mrs. W. D. McGraw
Mrs. Robert Rock

Mrs. Wanda Jackson
Mrs. J. W. James
Mrs. Walter Floyd
Mr. Bob Edd Shotwell
Mrs. C. T. Johnson
Mrs. Frances Leggett
Mrs. Belle Froelich
Mrs. Martha Ray
Mrs. Betty Arrell
Mrs. Dorothy Fleischauer
Mrs. Marilyn Berry
Mrs. Pat Harris
Mrs. Connie Harris
Mrs. Margaret Oliver
Mrs. Charlene Shipman
Mrs. Mary Gardner
Mrs. Blanca Herrera
Mrs. Virginia Kreimeyer
Mrs. Dora Roberts (2013-Present)

The Quarries of Hyde Park Baptist Church

The land for the Quarries has a very interesting story. One normal workday in the limestone quarry between U.S. 183 and MoPac Expressway, a man was down at the base of it using a bulldozer to move the loose rock; he broke into a natural spring. The water began gushing and filling the quarry so fast he just barely escaped with his life! The bulldozer is still down there, and now produces a nice sized natural lake.

Some time later, Texas Instruments Co. bought the quarry and surrounding property; built several tennis courts and had a nice recreation site for their employees. Economic times in the early 1980's caused the company to want to sell that property; some men from Hyde Park found out about it and helped the church acquire the Quarries. The Ralph and Bess Smith CLC was built, a football field and a baseball field were laid out, and someone stocked the lake with fish. Bess enjoyed the fishing!

In 2009, the Hyde Park High School was built, and the high school was moved from the Speedway campus. The School's cafeteria is now used as The Quarries Church and is growing every Sunday with new Christians being baptized frequently.

HYDE PARK'S MISSION STORIES

Bob Lumpkin
The comments about Bob were taken from the Weed-Corley-Fish Funeral Obituary page, and from Facebook.
-- Posted by: Peter Tadin - *Austin, TX* - Friend   Feb 11, 2014

Bob was bigger than life as he put Christ first in all he did. My very first memory of Bob was outside of the gym at 40th and Ave. F standing next to John Walters back in 1986. Bob was running the recreation ministry in addition to managing the Quarries; and John was his assistant. He worked tirelessly in reaching others through recreation and always tried to think new ideas to do this. In fact, he started the annual youth camp called Camp Travis, and the annual singles retreat called "Highlands." Both programs ran for 25 years or more. Bob also spearheaded steak dinners on Sunday nights after the evening worship service and attracted 50 or more singles on some nights. I also remember Bob getting the school bus and taking the singles out to the Coupland Inn for BBQ on a winter night several times. Bob also had a heart for missions and assisted John with several singles' mission trips working tirelessly as a carpenter, electrician, painter, and whatever else was needed from Mexico to Colorado helping small churches. One of my memories of Bob is of Bob telling a story of how Don Petter attempted to unclog a toilet in Mexico on a mission trip when the toilet didn't have any plumbing connected to it. When Bob's health started to decline, a single named Bert Hickman invited me to go with him in taking Bob out for dinner on a Thursday night, since Bob's eyesight was falling. Bert moved out of state; however, I kept picking Bob up at his apartment on Jollyville Rd. for 5 years every Thursday night to take him to dinner. Although he offered numerous times to pay for my dinner, we simply alternated in paying for each other's meal every week so the expense wasn't to become a burden to him. Yes, Bob came across gruff sometimes, but under his skin he was gentle and ever loving to those in need or less fortunate. I may have blessed Bob for 5 years, but the biggest blessing was mine to have crossed paths with him and I am better for it. Hyde Park had a man of God running the Quarries, the recreation ministry, and even part of the youth ministry if you count Camp Travis. I will always be grateful for the legacy he has left behind and look forward to seeing him again some day on the Streets of Gold, praising Jesus and singing "Blessed Assurance, Jesus in Mine."

Bob Lumpkin, March 2, 1938-February 7, 2014

DAK:

I just got word that the man who had the original idea and vision for Camp Travis, Bob Lumpkin, has passed on to be with the Lord. It is amazing to think about the 1000s of students he has influenced thru Camp Travis. He will be missed.

SKW: Little man by the window stood. Thanks Michael, can't get the song out of my mind now.

DAK @ TSP: -- Bob's health had been failing the last 4-5 years. He passed away about 3:00pm this afternoon due to congestive heart. He was 76, about to turn 77 next month. Arrangements are pending. Bob had been at the Windsor Nursing & Rehabilitation Center on Duval Rd. near the Quarries for about 5 years. He leaves behind a brother and his mom who is 99 years old and lives in a nursing home in Ft. Worth.

BR: When did this happen? He was my mentor! We won 6 championships for him and Hyde Park. Camp Travis made me the man I am today.

GB: Bob was so helpful in letting the youth from Texas Baptist Children's Home attend Camp Travis.

DR: Loved Bob! Such a great guy. What a great influence. Always made me feel special as a kid. Loved him. Will be a great reunion when I see him.

WD, Jr: Huge legacy.

GJ: Wow. Love that guy. He was a huge part of our young lives, and he didn't even get mad when we put his car seat on top of the concession stand at Camp Travis. Thankful for leaders like Bob when I was growing up.

AP: I love to eat those mousies. Mousies I love to eat. Bite their little heads off. Nibble on their tiny feet. (One of the songs Bob taught at Camp Travis.)

GB: In heaven's choir tonight the voice of Bob Lumpkin is being heard above all others!

SKB: Wow. He will always be remembered as a faithful servant for Christ. I know he is having quite the glorious celebration tonight.

Thanks for sharing this.

AEC: What a faithful servant of Christ. He has his new body in God's presence!

BCW: I have fond memories of him from the Camp Travis days. So sad to hear of his passing.

LSK: Beginning way back in the 70's he began our first weekly Youth Monday night Bible study and Camp Travis. A selfless worker always with a warm smile!

TC: I'll always remember the class he taught Baptist Faith and Message and the Sunday night singles supper RIP my friend.

RD: An amazing man I am so happy for him. He was an inspiration to me my whole life.

JK: I'm sorry to hear the news. I do miss his Bible studies and his advice.

RNW: I am very blessed to have known such a servant of the Lord's as he was... He is home now!!!

VBT with OG and 23 others

Today our mentor and friend, Bob Lumpkin, went home to be with Jesus! Just Wednesday night, he was singing Camp Travis songs with a friend, and today he had a glorious Homecoming just a month short of 77 yrs of age. So many of us have fond memories of Bob and his Ministry at the Quarries, Camps, etc.! We look forward to celebrating his life in the week to come.

Bob Lumpkin holding Tyler Tackett, 2001

John Walters with Bob Lumpkin in CLC

Betty Arrell

My story with Woman's Missionary Union begins on a Saturday morning, November 30, 1935. I was two days old. My father was pastor of a church near Whitney, Texas, and my mother was active in the woman's program.

Their group was called the Baptist Woman's Aid Society. Mostly what they did was to meet, to study the Bible, pray together, and minister in the community. WMU was not yet 50 years old. My father always said he would never pastor a church that did not have mission education to grow up a congregation to have a missions lifestyle, and to be informed about what the convention was doing, simply because a church that did not, would lack in two very important ingredients:

1. People would not be informed about the mission enterprise around the world and how to pray for them and

2. There would not be the atmosphere in the church out of which God would call his people to give and go.

The records show that even today most of our missionaries have received the call to go while they were members of RAs and GAs.

So I was born into the home of a mission minded pastor and wife. I was born at home, and two days later my mother had her woman's aid society at our home in Prairie Valley, Texas. I was too young to know what was going on as they gathered to study and pray under the quilt frame that hung in our living room, but what I do remember was many, many other times as I played on the floor beneath that frame where Godly women met to quilt and pray around the world. It was here that I first learned about my world.

I became a member of Sunbeams, where I first learned that Jesus wanted me to shine his light in a dark world, and then I was a GA where I learned my forward steps, and make the highest honor bestowed. Then it was on to YWA (Young Woman's Auxiliary.)

My grandmother, mother, and I learned to save the money we raised with the sale of vegetables, milk, eggs and it was set-aside for missions. In 1936, the record shows that the per capita given to missions among Southern Baptists, as a whole, was a meager $1.87, while woman of WMU at the same time gave per capita $4.49, in spite of the deep depression. In the years 1928-1936 the percentage of Home Mission Board was coming from WMU ranged from 59 to 91 percent of the board's total receipts.

It is not well known, but a fact, that WMU saved both mission boards, first from bankruptcy due to embezzlement (men connected with the board) and then from The Great Depression.

In l940 the SBC was deep in debt due to the embezzlement of funds and lack of giving during the depression and it was WMU that decided there would be a "Debtless Denomination by 1945. I was a Sunbeam then and each week we brought our pennies to help this cause. The convention debt was $3,000,000 and WMU would undertake to raise $1,000,000 of it. I remember my mother never let our church forget the words spoken by Charles Maddry, secretary of the Foreign Mission Board, when he said to the convention at large, "We will have our debts paid by l945. WMU has promised and we know we can count on them. Each woman was given this goal: "Debt free in '43, You can count on me" and so two years before the original date, when the final figures were tallied, WMU had given a full 61.2 percent of all the debt. Only eternity will show the blessings that will fall to every woman in WMU for giving and the souls won to the Lord with that money.

All my years growing up, our family vacations were to conventions, camps, or the WMU House Party. One highlight was in 1953, I was 18, and we traveled to Houston to celebrate 40 years of GAs and their leaders. If we were in a church where we had no adult leadership, my mother or father always kept the GAs and RAs going. I went off to college and was still a part of YWAs.

When Max and I married and I was working, there was no organization meeting at night and so for several years I missed out on my mission involvement, but God opened up a way for us to move to Austin in 1964 and we joined Hyde Park. One main motivating reason for young women to come to Baptist Women was due to the church providing free childcare for the meeting. This was before Mother's Day Out program. Another great contribution for WMU came when Bob Edd Shotwell came to the church. He saw to it that we had a budget to provide training, conventions, and all the things the Sunday School, and Music Ministry enjoyed. I have no idea what he had to go through to get that done from the deacons. He also fought for us and got the right for us to carry over money from our budget to another year so our Acteens could go abroad, which they are still doing. My family was blessed to be a part of Hyde Park during those glory days. Bob Edd was known through out the convention; Dr. Smith was a part of both the Foreign and Home Mission Board. Because of this our people were noticed, and I was asked to write for National WMU publications, to lead conferences at Baylor, Glorieta, and Ridgecrest, Jan Sutton, our Acteen Leader, and Judith Koon, our GA leaders were also asked to do these things.

Our organizations grew, and the entire church benefitted. My greatest honor was to be asked to be the Director of Hyde Park's WMU which I served for five years, and two of years (1987-1988) were the years leading up to the 100 year Celebration of WMU.
We took a large group to Richmond, Virginia, for the celebration.

Having gown up in a pastor's home, I am a product of Southern Baptist Life, been in church all my life, but there is no doubt the organization in my church that has the most profound influence has been WMU, far more than the music, the preaching, or Sunday School, for in WMU I have gotten music, Bible study, but it was in WMU that I saw the Great Commission come alive. It was in WMU I learned about the world, our need to cover that world with the knowledge that Jesus came to die for them. I was told we need to pray, give, and go tell them that Jesus came to save them, and that included me. It is WMU that has given me focus in my life and why I have spent my adult years in missions. This is my part of the story that must go on....

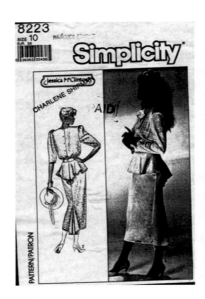

Charlene Shipman made the "period" dress for Betty Arrell to wear for the 100th anniversary of WMU. The quilt behind Betty is the commemorative quilt for the anniversary, made by Hyde Park WMU.

Evelyn W. Davison

God is Calling

The journey from Cut and Shoot, TX to Austin was long, sometimes difficult, and surely not planned.

Times were hard in the '30s for most of the people who lived there at the end of what was called the Big Thicket. Pine trees were everywhere, and the first game I remember playing, as a child was "kick the pine cone."

In my teen years, when World War II shook America, our family life was totally disrupted, and my dad closed our radio station when he was drafted into the Navy. We moved back to the piney woods where my grandparents lived. That part was God's blessing for us.

As a child, I had a major speech impediment, and was always fearful and insecure. It was a creative English teacher, whom God brought into my life, which brought help and hope. One day she looked at my weepy eyes and said, "Evelyn, you have some major disabilities, but, they don't have to have you." God used the mission heart of that teacher to bring change to my life.

One of our class projects was to write a three-act play. We called it, "God Is Always Able." We made puppets for the characters and performed it at luncheons to sell war bonds and at my teacher's church. Church had never been part of my family's life, but it was there at that small church I was introduced to Jesus, the Perfect One who loved me enough to give his life for me.

As I grew, I learned "perfect love casts out fear," and my life changed dramatically. I sought God's plan for my dreams. One dream was to be a foreign missionary. Years passed quickly into the college years, marriage and family.

To our surprise, in the late '60s, Van was transferred to Austin. I came, fearful and unhappy, but it did not take long for joy to return as God led us to Hyde Park Baptist Church.

It seemed more like Heaven for us than a mission field. When International Friendship was birthed by Bob Ed Shotwell, to my great surprise I realized I was a foreign missionary.

As years passed, other opportunities came to serve our Savior. Hyde Park was exciting and busy as we helped start twelve new churches.

Faith, hope and hard work opened a lot of doors: neighborhood Bible studies, radio, TV, National Day of Prayer, The Good News Journal, CLASS, and coaching and mentoring new Christians.

God is always able to do more than we think or dream — when we have a "mission heart." Excitement builds when we pray and seek him. He has a "Great Commission" for each of us.

"Co" means together. "Mission" means life or journey. As Jesus Followers, we are called to be his missionaries. It is simple: Get UP! Get OUT! Go TELL! That is this Great Commission He calls each of us to today.

God is calling: "Call ME and I will answer you and show great and mighty things which you have not seen." Jeremiah 33:3 LTV

To what mission is He calling you?

- Pray about it.

- Listen to him.

- Follow his way.

He is always able to do more than you can ever dream or imagine. He is doing that in my life.

© 2014, Evelyn W. Davison
Bio: Evelyn is America's Honorary Prayer Coordinator for National Day of Prayer, the founder of Love Talk Network, Publisher of Good News Journal and wife of Van Ed Davison, Austin Realtor.

HELEN HOY

I grew up in a Christian home. Our family attended worship service and Sunday School at Zion Lutheran Church in McGregor, Texas. As an infant I was sprinkled, the Lutheran form of dedication and infant baptism. I remember my mother attending a monthly meeting called the LADIES AID, which was a meeting where ladies made quilts, lap covers, etc. for someone—our "Mission Action" project. This is what I remember about missions at this time.

In my teen years when I began dating, my date (later my husband) took his sister and myself to youth functions at his church, which was Harris Creek Baptist Church. Times were hard at this time, no money to spend on dates, church functions were not costly. What better place for a date! As time passed, I attended more functions and services at his church. As I remember, I had really never heard the plan of salvation presented as I heard at this church. Several years passed and our relationship grew and we became engaged. I began to feel more of an urging to accept Christ as my Savior.

On a summer night in 1941, I gave my life to Christ at an outdoor revival held under a huge oak tree at Harris Creek Baptist Church. A week later, on a Sunday afternoon, I was baptized in Harris Creek. I still remember that day as if it just happened.

After my decision, my future husband and I talked with my parents. My parents were very encouraging. They said as a couple we needed to be in the same church. I have been blessed and active in a Baptist Church where we have lived.

We moved to Austin in1951 and joined Hyde Park in October 1951, and have been involved in many activities.

Our daughters were born in 1953 and 1957. They were both in the Sun Beams, directed by Eula Bolton, a lover of children and missions. They both attended all mission programs.

Because of a part-time position at the church, I was unable to attend the monthly mission programs, but I did attend a monthly circle meeting held at night. Later I was able to attend the monthly mission program which have all been informative and wonderful. I believe in missions, going into all the world to present God's love to all people—God's command to each of us.

May God bless the mission groups, the contributions and the trips God places on the hearts of our members.

Connie Harris
May 9, 2013

In the year 1985, I was asked by Betty Arrell, Sue Carlson and Belle Froehlich to be Baptist Women (that was what it was called then) president. At first I said, "No, thank you." I did not know that much about WMU or Baptist Women, even though I had grown up in Hyde Park and been through all the mission programs.

I learned real quick that you don't say no to those ladies, especially when sweet, southern Ms. Belle tells you that she had been praying and God told her to ask me. She then told me to "pray about it."

I didn't have a big problem saying no to God as much as saying no to Ms. Belle. So I accepted their invitation and became the youngest woman at age 27 to be BW president at HP. I believe I still hold that record today ☺

That summer, Betty and Sue talked me into attending the WMU conference in Ridgecrest. I was really nervous about going to the conference and attending the classes with so many "old" people, but after spending the week with Betty and Sue and other ladies, it was one of the best things I have ever done.

I learned so much at that conference in Ridgecrest. It was very encouraging to see other young women stepping up to the challenges of their churches. But more than that was the encouragement and support I received from my mentors.

After getting back to Texas, I was pretty excited and fired up to get started on changing the way that WMU was done. (I was young and naïve). I recruited several of my friends to serve with me as Mission Support and secretary. At first we were the blind leading the blind. Our mentors were gracious and kind and patient enough to let us try new things. With the help of the ladies, learning from our numerous mistakes and the grace of God, we made it through. I learned more than anything not to try to fix something that wasn't broke.

We had several young ladies that came to WMU that year. It was a great opportunity to start planting the seed and teaching those ladies about WMU and what missions meant to our church.

There is a growing interest and excitement here at HP to pray for missions, engage in mission action and witnessing, learn about missions and support missions more than ever before. With WMU leading the way, other mission opportunities have been created, like Great Destinations, Family Mission camp, Mission Austin, CUB (Church Under the Bridge), homes that have housed numerous missionaries on furlough, kid's missions, Friendship International and all of our departments from VBS, to Youth and Chapel Choir tours, to our mission trips that provide opportunities to go out and teach the great commission to others in our city and around the world.

I believe all these opportunities are because of the dedicated determination of WOM and I am proud and honored to have been a part of that mission.

Matthew 28:19 -20, "Therefore go and make disciples of all nations, baptizing them in the name of the Father and of the Son and of the Holy Spirit, and teaching them to obey everything I have commanded you. And surely I am with you always, to the very end of the age."

Judith A. Hiller

I was raised in a family that attended church and whose parents taught Sunday School, VBS and my mom conducted the choir and played the organ and piano. Church was a way of life. However, at aged 14, I heard Bill Graham speak and that night, as I read my Bible, which I was wont to do as I rolled up my hair before retiring, I was convicted in Corinthians about my own sin. I fell to my knees and confessed and prayed to receive Christ there at my bedside. I felt his power enter me and the burden of guilt rolled off me. I felt changed. The next morning I actually came out of my room to the kitchen and offered to help my mom. She was flabbergasted, as I never offered to help before that time. She wanted to know what had happened to me. I told her. I was fourteen years old at the time. I was baptized at our church a few weeks later. We were attending a Brethren Church in Maryland.

However, even though I was not born again until a teen, ever since I was in elementary school I have wanted to be a missionary and serve another language group of peoples. I began to learn Spanish in 5th grade to that end. I continued to study Spanish and majored in it at college eventually obtaining a Master's degree in Spanish linguistics.

Nevertheless, instead of becoming a full time missionary, I was married and produced our family. Yet, I served God and the church faithfully in many areas including Sunday School teacher for various grades for many years, and as a Vacation Bibles School teacher for over 40 years. I also served as church secretary in Laramie as well as their librarian. I have also served as an assistant director and director at Park Hills Baptist Church in Austin on the Living Nativity theatrical production with live animals and singers in a full dressed set and fully costumed actors for over 10 years.

Indeed, I have used my gifts and talents as a puppeteer, seamstress, production manager and singer for the church for over 50 years. I also lead Acteens at Park Hills in Milpitas, California as well as preaching and participating in the Prison ministry there.

Additionally, in Texas I have been involved in a ministry to international graduate students from the UT campus through our church. As well, I work with international ladies through a non-profit organization called Friendship International and have served in several capacities. I teach English as a Second language as well as Spanish to international students from all over the world. I have enjoyed using my talents and gifts for his kingdom be it language gifts or puppets. Through these ministries we have seen lives changed for Christ.

But it was not until I was in my 30's that I went on my first mission trip with my then church, Park Hills Baptist Church in Austin. I was working with the teens in a puppet ministry. We took puppets with us to minister to the children of the area. We flew into San Jose, California and then rented vehicles to drive to Fresno. We ministered to immigrant workers and their families. During the day, we conducted Vacation Bible Schools and during the night, services for the families at different homes in the area. I was able to use my Spanish and enjoyed connecting with the children especially. I told Bible Stories in their tongue.

Finally, I was a missionary to Spanish speakers! And I used my testimony in Spanish to reach the ladies and men I spoke to. And it was a joy to see God use my words, the life story he gave me, to reach and envelope others in his love.

My second mission trip was to the Brownsville area where we again, worked with Spanish speakers. I loved to connect with the children and women. Along with other ladies and some men, I went out in the neighbor hoods and spoke to families inviting them to a daytime backyard Bible club and the evening services. While the men worked on the target church rebuilding parts of it, renovating other parts, we ladies as well as teens, conducted Backyard Bible clubs complete with puppets and songs and other activities. I loved working with the people of that area, again utilizing my language skills, my compassion and love for the Hispanic people and the joy of the gospel.

My third mission trip was two weeks in Venezuela with an Evangelical International Organization. We arrived by plane, then took a bus for 8 hours into the interior to a small country town. We stayed at a pastor's home whose church it was that requested a team to come and help them with a revival and outreach program. We were assigned a team group with an interpreter.

When I was on the bus, however, I spoke Spanish fluently with the 30-year-old son of a Venezuelan pastor. We had a good time sharing what God is doing in the lives of his people. Because I could speak fluent Spanish, my husband, Paul and I were taken to a smaller village and left on our own with no other support but the members of the church! I was really kind of scared to be on my own and responsible to a church and its needs.

During that mission, though, God stretched me in many ways including language wise, faith wise and evangelization. I loved evangelizing in that area and doing so in Spanish. It is different here stateside because the personal space is 18 inches in the USA but it is very close in South America. As a result of this closeness, I could touch the ladies I was evangelizing and feel closer to them on all levels, breaking down the normal barriers one has in speaking the gospel. The close proximity and touch was crucial to sharing my heart and the word. All those to whom I spoke received Christ as their savior but for one woman who would not let us even come onto her property nor speak to her. There must have been over 17 people receive the Lord that two weeks. And that was only from my group-many more became believers in that town.

One woman, as we introduced ourselves, said she had been waiting two years to hear the gospel and speak to someone to ask Jesus into her life. This was so humbling to be used by God in this area. I saw him mightily at work among the people of Venezuela.

One afternoon, the pastor told me that he expected me to preach that night. Me, preach! What! Was this a joke? No, it was not. I prepared a sermon on faith-the three types: faith that God exists, faith that Jesus paid for our sins and makes us believers, and the faith that moves us in our daily walk as believers. I wrote out what I wanted to say and prepared my heart.

But I was nervous and found eating with butterflies in my stomach to be a trial. I do love to speak in front of a crowd, even to share my testimony and even to preach as I have done so in prisons where I serve in the jail ministry in California. But to preach in another language and to a mixed coed audience was mind blowing for me. And to top things off, they told me I had to wear a dress. And that the service would be outside. I was to stand on the bed of a truck and preach. Well, that was novel. Number one, I had no dress. So I wore a white tee shirt under a heavy nightgown that kind of looked like a longish knit dress. No one was the wiser for it. As I began to preach, I saw the stars overhead in the velvet expanse and felt filled with the Holy Spirit. I also saw bats diving and flitting about in the patches of light from the jerry rigged lights set up in the perimeter of the playground.

So. I preached and did so with vigor, logic and love--all in Spanish. When the service was over, one lady came up to me and said I did a good job, but only making one grammatical mistake-I used a masculine article with the word blood in Spanish. Oh well! Not too bad for my first time to preach in a foreign language and in my nightgown!

My third mission trip was to China. Here, God took me from the familiarity of the language and land into a completely different continent, language and culture. Paul and I flew into Beijing airport and then took a hop to the south to the Yunan peninsula. We went to a university to conduct camps on leadership training with Chinese students. We had small group times in which we lead discussions and participated in games and activities.

The jet lag was a killer for me as well as the food. The food was a problem for me because I am highly allergic to MSG-that is monosodium glutamate. If any of you get headaches at Chinese restaurants from the food, it is most likely that MSG is the culprit. For me, it is more than a headache; it triggers myoclonic dyskinesia. This is a condition in which, due to a chemical trigger or a light or pattern trigger, causes a misfire in my brain. To compensate, the brain sends the electrical impulses into the muscles of the body. Therefore, I jerk and spasm. Not fun, and the more MSG in the food, the greater the jerking. Myoclonic means over all the body, dyskinesia mean jerking. So I am a real jerk. It also affects my breathing and I get very asthmatic. So combine the myoclonic situation from the food, the high elevation with my heart arrhythmia and asthma and we get a lady who was having a hard time in China ministering to others when she had to minster to herself! But this allowed others to minister to me and pray over me and help. However, God used me regardless of my health situation. We saw over 30 students saved during those two weeks out of 200 students.

Our second trip to China the following year was in Xian, which is more central and lower in elevation. My heart worked better and I had no asthma. I ate only rice and fruit. I brought peanut butter and nuts with me so I felt well. God used us again to reach out to and minister to Chinese students. In my group of 8 students, only 2 did not want to become believers. One fellow, Jack, was so hurt as a child not only physically but also emotionally. He had never been loved nor felt any love. That God loved him enough to die made a big difference in his life. And he became a believer.

The camp is one that teaches leadership skills and is supported by the government and Chinese Red Cross. We teach leadership skills based on the sacrificial leader-and ultimately this points to Jesus. In their culture, the leader is served and the people are secondary. But in the leadership courses we taught, it is reversed. This made a big impact on all the students. In addition to the group times and lectures, American leaders are expected to teach courses in the afternoon. I taught a course on public speaking which was so much fun! Again, this class gave me an "in" with the students and drew us closer so that I could share my faith.

So I have reached my goal of being a missionary to Spanish speakers. But in reality, God has gone beyond my puny expectations and taken me to far off Asia. Further, and perhaps more amazing, I do not need to leave my city because he brings the internationals to my city so I can minister here in Austin. As my friend Joyce Parker says, "I can be a missionary in the morning and home for lunch in the afternoon!" God is greater than our grandest dreams. He gives us visions; He fulfills those visions and then turns about and gives us new ones. God is great in deed!

Janis Mather

I was reared by a grandmother and mother who thought that every woman should be in WMU. Finally, when I was able to participate in WMU, I participated. To me, that was what I needed to do and wanted to do.

When I was a small child, I was put in day care while my grandmother and mother attended WMU. While I was in school, there was no way I could attend WMU. Then I was off to college and then to a teaching career. After teaching a while, I returned home and spent another year back in school. After that, I spent 31 years working at The University of Texas and then retired. During this time, I met a young man that my parents and I were able to lead to the Lord. We have now been married over 45 years.

In the process of time, my father died. Eventually my husband and I and my mother all came together at Hyde Park Baptist Church. After joining Hyde Park, my mother and I felt we should join WMU at Hyde Park. At this time I was helping with the food service in the church kitchen. There became a need for someone to help with the WMU lunch each month, so I volunteered to do that. As I helped get the lunch together, my dear mother knitted caps while she waited for lunch and for WMU to start. She knitted thousands of caps that went with mission trips from church around the world. There are pictures of people wearing these caps.

So at Hyde Park Baptist Church, I found a niche for me. I love my place in the WMU organization. I'm glad I can help out.

MINEOLA GRUMBLES

On 4"x6" cards, class members wrote a note to Mineola Grumbles expressing their appreciation, thoughts and prayers for her. The cards were put into an album and presented to her at the May First, 2010, Tuesday Mission Luncheon Meeting. (This album is in the WMU closet, 2nd floor of the HPBC West building.)

Mineola Grumbles began UT at the age of 42, attending classes with her daughter, Janis. She then taught English at Austin High School. She taught Adult SS from 1981 to 2005, worked in WMU and Women on Mission through Church Under the Bridge, Baptist Community Center, Soup Kitchen, VBS, and wrote notes for GROW (God Rewards Our Work), and served in the Prayer Ministry twice a week. She knitted 400 caps a year for several years; these caps were sent with our various mission trips from Hyde Park. At 96 years of age, this was still her goal. The countries that have received these caps include Mexico, Latvia, Sudan, Romania, Paraguay, Asia, and North America.

WHAT WILL YOU BE DOING WHEN YOU ARE 96 YEARS OLD

Eldon and Catherine Bebee

Eldon and Catherine met at Hyde Park Baptist Church and then stayed here serving The Lord for the next 57 years. Their love for Christ was exhibited as he served as Chairman of the Deacons and was on the Sanctuary Building Committee and in the prayer ministry. He also served on both the Baylor University and the Baptist Foundation Board of Trustees. He had a successful banking career, was president of North Austin State Bank, and was instrumental in the financing of the new sanctuary. He had a part in the acquisition of the Quarries property and development of it.

Catherine used her sewing talents by making Christmas stockings for her four children, their children and their children. She also made decorated pillowcases for her friends, and made many clothing outfits for the children of the River Ministry of Mexico. She said this proves "a stitch in time saves nine." She sewed love into many other projects.

Catherine's life ministry was to express God's love in word and deed to countless children at the Baptist Community Center for more than 40 years. She served faithfully on the board of the Texas Baptist Children's Home in Round Rock, Texas. She was an active member of Hyde Park Baptist Church where she taught Sunday School for 50 years, served in Women's Missionary Union, actively partnered with Eldon in the Prayer Ministry begun by her son, and served in countless other ministries.

Catherine and Eldon leave a legacy of faithfulness to Christ, their family, and their church, of what really matters—the glory of God!

Lattie Phelps

From memoir written sometime after 1966

Regarding faith in her family during her childhood:

We went to Liberty School for the religious services. Papa went early because he felt he had to get the building in order for church services by dusting, cleaning, trimming the wicks of the coal oil lamps, lighting the fires and other chores. Women had very little part in the services – they were to be seen and not heard.

In our home, our religious life was a part of everything, every day. Our family life was the most consistent Christian living I knew. I make no apology for making this statement. When I visited girlfriends occasionally during school years, never did they have family prayer and/or scripture reading or expressing thanks at meals. Mama was a Christian when she and Papa married; but Papa was saved at age 29 years of age and lived a dedicated life thereafter. He was a deacon during all of my life. Mama would pray at home, but she was shy and did not often pray in public. We attended the little Baptist church about 2-1/2 miles from home, near Vashti, Texas. Papa went one night and knelt to pray. A scorpion was in his shoe and stung him as he was praying…he said it cut his prayer rather short!

Added note: a memory from Joyce Parker.

After Lattie was married and had children, her daughter, Mary Sue, told me, "Mother was always involved in WMU and would leave us at home during that time. She also sang in the choir and controlled us with a stare that scared us into behaving!"

Two of Lattie's daughters, Mary Sue Carlson Parker and Belle Froelich, were active members of the Hyde Park Baptist Church WMU in the 1960s and 1970s. Sue was on the Mission Study committee; Belle was one of the presidents of the Hyde Park Baptist Church WMU.

In 1965 Lattie gave her testimony during the musical "The Longer I Serve Him" led by Joe Carrell, Minister of Music. Joyce Mott sang the song by that same name written by Bill Gaither.

The following photographs are of Lattie Phelps and her daughters and friends in Hyde Park.

At a WMU meeting, October 1994

Oliver and Mary Elaine Carlson, Sue
Carlson Parker, Frances McGraw

Latttie Phelps and her daughters

Sue Parker and Marge Snowden

MARY GARDNER, MY MISSIONS STORY

As a young girl, I listened to my Grandma tell of her adventures riding the bus over to East Austin each week to teach Bible stories and sing Bible choruses with the little children who lived in that area. As I got older, she asked me to go with her, and she would let me lead the songs and help with the craft time and she would tell the flannel graph Bible story. That was my first experience with missions, and one that has made an indelible impact on my life. I have always had a heart for missions since that time.

I attended a Christian college that encouraged our doing missions ministry on Saturday mornings, and I went out with a group of students many Saturdays and conducted neighborhood and playground Bible clubs. When I served as Division Director at Hyde Park, we started conducting Mission VBS's in the summers with kids from disadvantaged neighborhoods who we would bring in by bus. Our Minister of Education even started Bible clubs in East Austin, and I helped with those for a year or two.

It wasn't until after retiring from teaching that I was able to become more actively involved in Hyde Park's WMU ministry, serving in various capacities, including the Christian Women's Job Corps support group, and serving as WMU Director. While I was Director, WMU organized and its leadership led a mission trip to Juarez for several summers, which was my first—and my only—missions trip outside the United States.

I remember vividly a mission's commitment service at a college chapel service where I told the Lord that I was willing to go to a foreign field in fulltime service if He called me. I very definitely sensed that He would not need me there, but He always wanted me to be available here for whatever tasks He might call me to do. That is what I will always plan to do.

Shyrell Anne and Dick Van Arsdale

The Downtown Learning Center of the Brooklyn Tabernacle

This mission effort began in the summer of 2006, while Shyrell Anne and I were in New York City, and attended a Sunday service at the Brooklyn Tabernacle, which featured a commencement ceremony for several people, who received their GED diplomas. These people attended the Downtown Learning Center, which is sponsored by the Brooklyn Tabernacle, and is free to anyone who wants to complete their GED requirements. While there was a small administrative staff for the school, all of the tutors were volunteers, who wanted to help the students attain their goals.

There were many heartwarming stories about the graduates and, during the ceremony, we decided that we would explore being volunteer tutors. So, after the service, we went across the street and inquired about what the qualifications were to serve in the Learning Center. In the ensuing weeks, we had other conversations with the Center Staff and then decided that we would get our affairs in order and move to New York to teach at the school. So in the summer of 2007, we rented an apartment in New York for the fall semester, and moved there to volunteer as tutors.

Classes were offered from 9am-noon, 1-4pm, and 6-9pm. We each had classes for the morning and afternoon sessions, with class sizes of 15-20 students. The school had about 900 total enrolled, and the ages ranged from about 16 to mid-60's. The classes were similar to one-room schoolhouses, as each student had dropped out of high school, so each class had considerable age differences within the classes. Most of the females in the younger age groups had dropped out of school because they got pregnant, or were kicked out of school for fighting, as it seems fighting among girls in Brooklyn is common! There was much one-on-one working with them, as each of them was in a different place in their education and understanding. Same for the males.

For the young men, it was drugs, or it was part of their sentencing for other petty crimes. The students were largely minorities, and there were many islanders who had immigrated to the United States with most of the students on some sort of government subsidies; although, many had some sort of job. However, some of the older students were just normal working people who just wanted to go back and get their GED's. A GED to them was like a Doctorate to us, and was viewed as a major accomplishment.

There were many stories to tell, and most of them were really heart wrenching because of their circumstances. It was very difficult to keep focused, knowing some of their stories, but it was all part of what we were called to do there----not just to teach them, but to love them. We were originally told not to touch the students, but Shyrell Anne is a "hugger," and soon all of our students became huggers also!

This all began once the students figured out that we were there to really help them. It was routine for many churches around the country to make one week "mission trips" to help out at the Learning Center where a group would come in and essentially "help" the tutors, but in reality, being there for a week in the middle of a semester didn't accomplish much, and the students viewed the visitors as "some church group just getting their merit badges" so they could return to their churches and talk about all the great work that was done. And the first few days the students weren't very accepting of us, as they viewed us as "some white southerners dropping in" for the reasons mentioned above. But once they learned that we had moved there and planned to spend several months, everything changed and they essentially "let us into their worlds;" and from that point on, our classes evolved into real relationships with the students so that they didn't just feel like bodies sitting in a classroom. We all became "family."

Shyrell Anne taught geometry, writing and critical thinking while I taught geometry, percentages, and fractions; and we essentially created our own lesson plans, with subjects that reflected the things the students would deal with in their everyday lives.

Each day our class sessions ended with prayer. It was a joy to share the love of God with people who so often felt, and were treated, as though there was nothing about them to love. We were blessed to be able to pray with folks from all faiths and many with no faith at all.

We returned in the summer of 2009 to attend the graduation ceremony and were able to see some of our students get their GED's.

Our time there was probably the most rewarding time of our lives, and we had discussed someday returning there to teach again; but unfortunately, when the financial meltdown occurred in 2008, the Downtown Learning Center was a casualty, and it closed in 2009.

Frank and Gladys Keathley
(Taken from her obituary autobiography)

Gladys and Frank and their family moved to Austin in 1963. They joined Hyde Park Baptist Church, he taught Math at McCallum High School and she took the Civil Service exam and became a tax examiner for the IRS. They both worked in the children's Sunday school and choir. Frank played the piano and she also sang alto in the Sanctuary Choir. She taught second grade Sunday school for 20 years.

After Gladys retired in 1980, she taught English as a second language on Sunday evenings, played in the Handbell Choir, and played volleyball until she fractured her ankle. She was also in Friendship International of Austin and WMU. While in WMU, she helped with the birthday parties in nursing homes.

She wrote her Christian Testimony in 1978. "I was an unsaved Methodist who thought all my righteousness assured me a place in heaven. After I married, my husband discovered after a few 'religious' discussions that I wasn't truly saved. He had people praying for me. Shortly afterward, during a Baptist revival, the Holy Spirit opened my eyes; it was as if I had been blind and now could see. It was the happiest day of my life to know that I was going to heaven and to know it didn't depend on my works or lack of them. I now know that my conversion was the most wonderful life-changing thing God ever did for me."

EDITOR'S NOTE: Frank was giving his tithing testimony one February Sunday and taught us how to figure what a tenth is. Remember, he was a math teacher. He taught us "you take the big number, not the small number, and you move the decimal point over to the left one place, and that is the amount you write on your tithe check." I heard someone near me say, "Now I get it!"

Carol Hance, Mission Trip to Juarez

Dictated to Linda Everton

In 2005 and 2006, a mission group, including a number of WMU members, traveled to a barrio (Spanish word meaning neighborhood.) outside of Juarez to work with an orphanage and a poverty-ridden barrio on the Mexican border. The group helped construct and roof a building for the barrio to house a church. They carried clothing and goods to help the group and the orphanage. The members stayed at the orphanage inside Juarez, rather than in the neighborhood, and the mission group conducted vacation bible schools in the neighborhood and at the orphanage. Hyde Park members gathered clothing to deliver. Hyde Park-ers included: Julia Petter, Henry and Bee Klingemann, Jim and Charlene Shipman, Laura Herrera, Rachel West and her sister, Ruby, Pat Stivers, Zuleima Martinez, Stacey and Jose Figueroa, Sherrie and Jose Correa, Francois and Diego Newkirk, Taylor Anne and Kim King, Mary and Dan Gardner, Craig and Lydia Gonzales, Trisha and Steve Belknap, Grace and Yolanda Perez, and Carol Hance.

Jewell Rossback

SUDAN

When I was a young child attending First Baptist Church in Taft, Texas, a couple that were missionaries in Africa would come to our church and tell us many, many stories about Africa. I was in GA's and this couple came and talked to us about what they did as missionaries in Africa. It became my dream that one day I would go to Africa and do mission work.

Praise God, at the age of 60, I finally went. After much prayer, I felt God was calling me to go and tell His Word. I thought to myself, but God, what do I have to do to do this? I just felt I had nothing to give these people. I got on the plane thinking "Why, God, did you choose me"? We landed in Nairobi, I was really anxious; "Why God did you choose me"? I remember when we got to Sudan my anxiety was removed. I felt a sense of why God sent me to Africa. The CHILDREN. God's love and His Holy Spirit were with me.

There was Jane Gunn and I working with the children. The Holy Spirit was everywhere we went. Our first day with the children, there were over 500 children. It was almost overwhelming. But with God doing everything, it was wonderful. The young girls and boys, at first, could not hold down their excitement and would rush to see us. They wanted to touch us, hold our hands and just look at us. These children became my children, but foremost, they were Children of God. We told stories, which in Africa, story telling is common. This is how they talk to each other. There was no electricity, no running water. These people would sit around a fire at night telling stories.

My trips to Sudan were amazing, working with the young children. We spent our days singing, playing games and telling the amazing stories from the Bible. We danced and prayed. We prayer walked around the village. One lady we visited with was very ill and could hardly walk. Even though she had difficulty walking, she would meet us at a place for church at 4 p.m.

When it would rain, we would put on our mud boots and go and be with the children. It sometimes took us a couple of hours to get to them, but God always had a path ready for us to get to them. There were many children that had never heard about Jesus. They were eager to hear the stories about our Lord Jesus from the beginning of time to when Jesus died to take away our sins. Many days, the mothers would come with the children, to also learn the Good News.

We would have moments of tears for the children as we felt their love for us, their eyes of so much need and so little food. There were also times of laughter as we played games and danced. They taught us music they sang and dances they danced. I have to admit at the age of 60 it was hard to do some of them.

In the evenings, we would sit under the stars and share our meals with our interpreters. Just to listen to them talking in their language was music to my ears. I am so blessed to have been given this opportunity to go to Africa. In the years I went, there were many children that accepted our Lord Jesus as their Savior. God had faith in me when I did not. Thank You, Jesus, for granting me this opportunity.

I also want to say thank you to Bill, my husband. He stayed here supporting me in prayer, taking my calls in the middle of the night. Bill was my best supporter and my best encourager when I felt tired and sometimes spiritually drained. I thank God for giving me this man to live my life with.

I also thank Hyde Park Exaltation choir. Your music was played when we got up every morning to eat breakfast and before our daily prayer time. At night, when we would come back to camp, we listened to the music before bedtime. You were there with us on each and every trip we went on. I also want to thank our church for supplying so many things for the children and adults. The children had never seen balloons, crayons, pencils, candy, jump ropes, etc. THANK YOU.

There have been many interpreters that have become leaders and minister to other villages. Some even started Christian schools. They have little support financially but the Grace and Love of God in their hearts wanted to continue to spread the Good News even in times of fear for life. I ask you, please, to pray from them.

I will not see the children again until we meet in heaven. What joy that will be!

Robert and Jane Gunn

As a boy, I learned about missions from my parents and from my church. I belonged to the Royal Ambassadors (RA's) from the earliest badge through Ambassador Plenipotentiary – the focus in all those years was Missions. I attended church camp each summer. There was always a focus on Missions. My mother served as WMU President on some occasions. The WMU was highly focused on Missions. As early as ten years of age I was thinking about Africa. I remember even now (65 years later) the book about an African boy my age. He loved to allow ants or termites to crawl in his throat before he swallowed them. That would excite any boy about going to Africa.

Fast forward to 2003 when I arrived in Uganda on my first mission to Africa. I remember standing on that ground and weeping for JOY! I had the strange feeling of being home. It felt natural. I had not been running in disobedience from the Lord concerning Missions. I was a part of the first Partnership Mission in the early 70's. First we went to Soporo, Japan. The next year we went to Casteon de la Plana, Spain. Then later Jane and I were in Budapest, Hungary and in Uruapen, Mexico and on a Medical Mission on the Amazon River. Now, after 19 missions to Africa, I (we) can affirm our total commitment to being "used up" in our calling to the Toposa Tribe of South Sudan.

The Toposa is a tribe of perhaps 750,000 unreached and unengaged people. The IMB had stated they had no plan nor knew of any other organization with plans to reach this people. Along with Larry Riley, representing Hyde Park Baptist Church, and under the leadership of e3 Partners Ministry, we launched our first Mission in September of 2007 when a team of 11 stood at the edge of a village of this tribe realizing that we were called to that spot at that moment, yet we had no translators. We were among a people who were uneducated – who had no Bible in their language – and we had no local leader to follow. Using a satellite telephone, we called our prayer captain in Austin and asked for the prayer team to present our request to the Lord for 6 translators. The next day before noon we had six translators who spoke very good English (for our benefit) and could communicate very well with the Toposa Tribe. Our calling to the Toposa was confirmed. We have been certain since those first hours that we should be a part of the movement that is needed among this large group.

We have now completed 11 missions to this area. We have partnered with Patricia Caroom who is a coordinator of church planting with e3 Partners. I joined e3 Partners as an Associate Staff after retiring from my business in 2008. For the past few years we have partnered with John Wanyoni, a Baptist Missionary Pastor from Kenya. More recently, Pastor Stephen Lobolia and his family from Kenya have joined with us in this blessed ministry. Large numbers have received the Lord. In our Mission last May, 19 received believer's baptism – many others have been baptized throughout this past year. Eight young men began as boys under the Children's ministry of Jane along with Sam Kpakima (Children in Christ, Kenya). These young men have reached the point that they are now regularly sharing the gospel through Bible Studies that they conduct at the schools they attend some distance away from their home and the base of our ministry. Many are receiving Christ and churches are being planted. We feel that a movement has begun. We have already begun 2nd generation churches and are praying for the planting of a 3rd generation church in November 2013. This means that the beginning church planted a church, which planted a church. Through multiplication (not addition) we believe we will reach Christ's mandate concerning His return. He said (Mt 24:14) "And this gospel of the Kingdom will be preached in the whole world as a testimony to all nations, and then the end will come." What a JOY to be a small part in His Return!

Two for Sure,
Robert and Jane Gunn

Helen Brown

At the age of eighteen I accepted Jesus Christ as my personal savior at a revival in the state of Illinois where my family lived. A short time later my family moved to Tucson, Arizona. It was in Tucson where I met my husband to be, Jim Brown. We married a few months later and eventually had three children. I was blessed to be a stay-at-home mom.

My husband's work brought us to Austin, Texas. Eleven years later my husband became ill and he went to be with the Lord. We had three teenagers and felt I needed to go back to work, which was good for me at that time in my life.

I had never participated in the different church activities except Sunday School Class, and was invited to attend the Dickson/Oliver evening mission group, and then I became a member. Next, I attended a monthly luncheon and was impressed by the many mission projects the evening group and the monthly luncheon group were involved. To me this was fulfilling the great commission. I was asked to help with the luncheon group as table hostess, which I was happy to accept. It has been a joy listening to, giving money to, and praying for those who go on the mission trips. I do that and believe that all churches should be mission churches.

Margaret Rightmire Pettit

My story seems rather insignificant. I have not been on mission trips, per se, even though I have traveled quite a bit going back and forth to California, where I grew up, since I was fifteen years old—many times by bus, later by train and air.

In recent years, I have made some great trips to points in the United States with the German Choir I sing with. Two trips to Germany and one to Paris, France with my family in the last three years were the most exciting of all. I do not consider myself an evangelist, don't know for sure if I have led anyone to the Lord, but my many years as a Nurse presented many, many opportunities to witness, which I have done. I feel this was how God used me to show my patients, their families and fellow workers how important my faith is to me.

I have been a member of Hyde Park for about nine years, formerly a member of Congress Avenue Baptist Church and Wyldwood Baptist Church. I have three children which were raised Methodist, but now all three attend the Baptist Church. I have five granddaughters and three great-grandchildren; all live in Central Texas.

Julia Petter

To Julia Petter, WMU is a large part of her life. Since 1992, when on her first life changing international mission trip to most recently, where she teaches preschool children in a number of ways. From teaching in Community Bible Study, leading Clubhouse Worship, writing Curriculum for any number of Church activities and utilizing her Seminary Education to teach children about the Lord.

Taking numerous trips abroad, the WMU has invited Julia to share her experiences at various Mission Lunches and Dinners. Those trips included Argentina, China, the UK, Honduras, Zimbabwe, Russia, Sweden, Mexico, Scotland and along with the first; France and Spain. These trips included sports ministry, construction, VBS, mentoring and evangelism.

The enthusiasm with which the information was shared and received allowed Julia to serve as the Missions Coordinator for the WMU from 1997 thru 2002. As a recipient of the WMU Eula Mae Henderson Scholarship, afforded the opportunity to complete a Masters Degree in Christian Education from Southwestern Baptist Seminary in 2001.

This education has enabled Julia to carry on the purpose of the WMU; to educate and involve preschoolers, children, youth, and adults in the cause of Christian missions. Whether home or abroad, the goal of WMU is not simply a part-time hobby or interest, it is a calling; a way of life that encourages all involved to serve the Lord to the best of their ability.

In any given situation, it is possible to educate and involve anyone and everyone in the cause of Christian missions. Praying, financial support to missions, traveling on mission, and providing resources for mission trip activities are some of the ways to involve others.

Lastly, the Hyde Park WMU has been an organization like no other. Some of Julia's dearest and closest friends come from their mutual involvement in WMU. On a more personal note, the birth of a miracle child to Don and Julia Petter in 1999 and with the assistance of the WMU ladies has taught Julia that the Lord provides us with the desire to know Him more deeply. The WMU women at Hyde Park Baptist church prayed for, assisted with, and taught Julia countless ways to serve the Lord in raising her son. Upon acceptance of the Eula Mae Henderson scholarship while in seminary, Julia committed to use the knowledge acquired to help educate and involve the people around her. This includes son Duke, along with any and all people that the Lord sends her way. For this, Julia is forever grateful.

The WMU is what people make of it, and at Hyde Park Baptist Church the Lord uses this organization to achieve the Great Commission. "Therefore go and make disciples of all nations, baptizing them in the name of the Father and of the Son and of the Holy Spirit, and teaching them to obey everything I have commanded you. And surely I am with you always, to the very end of the age." Matthew 28:19-20

Mary Beth Fleischer
SEPTEMBER 2013
Dictated to Julia Petter one week before Mary Beth's Home-going

Mary Beth Fleischer recalls WMU programs at her church in West, TX, in 1934 thru 1938. Her first exposure, called "Sunbeams," was the youngest group, went until WWII broke out.

Sarah Hankins was her first teacher in SS who became the GAs, or "Girls in Action," director after WWII. YWA, or "Young Women in Action," preceded the modern day "Acteens" equivalent. Young ladies in WYA were not active until attending college, whereas, today's Acteen participates as soon as they enter teenage years.

Mary Beth became a YWA after college in Pleasanton, TX, at the encouragement of her friends Jerry Lynn and Mary Helen Campbell. Their mom was active in WMU and as a result, the young ladies were as well. During 1955-60, Mary Beth became more familiar with WMU. She moved to Ft. Stockton during the early 60's and participated there as well.

While in college at North Texas Women's in the 60's and the Campbells attending Baylor, the three friends attended an out of town WMU State Convention trip; much to the dismay of her Mother. They attended and lived to tell about it, and other State conventions. These trips taught Mary Beth a great deal more about WMU in a first-hand manner.

After retirement, Mary Beth became active in WMU and participated in the first Tuesday Mission Luncheons. She had not attended these Luncheons during employment due to work schedules. With numerous ladies in the same situation of working and not to be hindered, the late Dorothy Fleischauer, Mary Beth, Norma Wiggins, Edna Sparks, Carolyn Kay, Lynda Conway, Arlene Ulrich and Betty Turner began a second Tuesday evening WMU dinner. The Marlene Barger, Kathy Harper and the Tracy Adair groups were just some of the names used.

The dinner was held at the Fleischer home so that her sickly mother could be a part of the group and learn more about Missions. The group was re-named the Dickson-Oliver group. It was to honor specific former Missionary Families. It later joined another group also named after Missionaries, on and off the field.

Other groups Mary Beth involved herself in thru the WMU include the Nina Pinkston Nursing home group, which visited patients at Buckner Villa to celebrate Birthdays and provide Christian fellowship. The Harris Roundtable read Christian books, reviewed and provided discussion and exchange of knowledge. Additionally, Mary Beth supported the Christian Women's Job Corps. This organization provided training and various resources to women in need of assistance to provide for themselves and their families. Teaching English as a second language in Friendship International as well as assisting in the Nursery with the children allowed Mary Beth to experience Missions first hand.

Although Mary Beth became more active with WMU after retirement, she learned a tremendous amount about missions. She was compelled to support Missions, Mission groups and Missionaries. Her age was not a hindrance in her service to the Lord.

Joyce van Ermel Scherer
2013

God's Word needs to be shared.

Because Bob (van Ermel Scherer) is a member of The Gideons International, I was able to join the Auxiliary. The Auxiliary has prayer meetings to ask God to guide the Gideons and Auxiliary to bring His Word into the World.

Recently the Auxiliary had distributions in July and August to Doctors' & Dentists' Offices and there was a need for Bibles and New Testaments for the Medical Personnel.

After the distribution in July, the ladies went for lunch to Luby's and when we were seated, I sensed that the waitress had a problem and I gave her "a present," a pocket New Testament and showed her where she could find help and also to read the Plan of Salvation. She accepted the Testament and said: "Thank you" and went on with her work. A few minutes later, she came back and gave me a big hug and said, "How did you know that I needed this?" "God nudged me to give it to you."

On August 1, after we had a very exciting distribution, we stopped at Luby's again and when this waitress saw me sitting with my friends, she came to me and said, "Thank you again for giving me that testament, my daughter reads it every day. Do you by any chance have 5 Spanish Testaments?" And guess what? Those were the only 5 Testaments that we had left. Be alert to what God wants you to do and souls might be saved.

This is just an example of what the Auxiliary work is all about.

May God guide us with ExploreGod.com. To Him be the praise and the glory.

Darlene May

FRIENDSHIP MEMORIES

During our showing of the Jesus video, one of the ladies from Iran asker her American friend, "How much does the church pay you?" When she answered that she worked in Friendship as a volunteer, the woman looked very puzzled. "You must get money –you bring me to church each week and you teach me." When the friend responded again that she did this because God loves us and wants us to love others, the Iranian lady looked up to the sky and said, "One day God will write you a check."

After sitting with the Iranian ladies to the see the Jesus Film in Farsi, one woman remained after the others had left. I'll never forget looking at her tear-stained face as she asked me, "Who is this Jesus?"

A Japanese student of mine returned home after being in Austin for one year. While here, she attended Friendship classes and was a faithful member of the International Sunday School Dept. We received an e-mail telling us that she had found an ESL teacher so she could keep improving her English and that she had found a church! Those planted seeds are being watered!!!!

Nancy Hill was a Japanese war bride who settled in Austin. After some time, she became a Christian and a very active member of Friendship. Nancy was always at the Registration Table each week and also taught Citizenship. I remember talking to her one morning and she told me she had finished making a quilt….all by hand. What a wonderful thing to have and to treasure I told her! She replied to me that she had given it to her Sunday School teacher. Again, what a treasure…and what did her teacher think about the gift? Nancy said she laid the quilt on her desk before class began. When her teacher came into the room she questioned everyone…"Who made this beautiful quilt?" No one knew anything about it. When she quizzed Nancy, her response was, "What does Japanese know about 'kilting'?" That was Nancy, always doing for others!

I have been in Friendship since 1970 and there are many memories tucked inside my head.

Robert Horan

Samuel Clintoc (formerly on staff at HPBC, now Park Hills Baptist Senior Pastor) led a group of 5 Hyde Park men to Romania.

Samuel met us at the Budapest airport with a van and then we rode together across the border into Romania towards our destination - Oradea. Oradea is home to Emanuel University and Seminary. Emanuel is a unique school because it marries Christian education across all disciplines; for example, future pastors have to take business classes, and future businessmen have to take theology classes. The school campus is well designed, practical and comfortable. Emanuel has an impressive roster of friends, including Dr. Adrian Rogers, Dr. Paige Patterson, and Dr. Walter Elwell.

If I have to distill down the entire trip to a few summary points, the main point would be the commonality of our experiences. Whether we are following God in Texas, Romania or elsewhere, our challenges, pain and victories are often much the same.

If you have ever had lots of disappointments in life, or if that pain is still particularly raw and fresh, in Romania you will certainly find someone with whom you can share your story, relate to, and encourage. One such Christian lady lived on the top floor of a tall apartment building (it is cheaper at the top because there was no elevator) and we were bringing her some bags of groceries. Hers was a particularly sad story. She was recently widowed and dealing with the grief of that acute loss. But then to compound the difficulty, her son abandoned his children, leaving them with her, not giving her any money to care for his children, neither giving her any emotional support in raising his children in his place. The grief was palpable. The need was clearly visible and her pain was strong. I had been going through a time of loss in my life and could relate to her feelings of abandonment and wondering if God had somehow forgotten about me. It is an interesting thing, that when you have experienced a significant pain, you can look someone deep in the eyes, and with only a few words, express Christian camaraderie and encourage a fellow Christian that no, no, no - God had not forgotten her. Through the shared tears, you can remind a suffering saint of God's promises and share what God has done in your life. Even though things may not change soon, there is somehow comfort in knowing that another saint understands what you're going through and can remind you that God is still at work, even when you can't quite see what He's been up to yet, and to cling once again to His promises.

We spent some time with some of the seminary students. What was most impressive were their testimonies. One young man, in particular, demonstrated what it is like to give your all for God. He comes from a poor family and has vision problems. For school, he has to read a lot of books, but the more he reads, the more it hurts his eyes. He loves to read the Bible, but wishes that there was a way for him to read his Bible and not hurt. Yet, to fulfill the mission God had called him to, he has to read through his pain.

You can find more information about Emanuel University and Seminary at www.emanuel.ro/en.about

Joann (Reynolds) Traver And George Traver

"A Sunbeam, a Sunbeam, Jesus wants me for a Sunbeam,

A Sunbeam, a Sunbeam, I'll be a Sunbeam for Him."

In GA's the song was "We've a Story to Tell to the Nations" and every time we sing that today I think of GA's.

I was fortunate to be born into a Christian family. My parents, **Gladys and Robert Reynolds**, were very active at Hyde Park even at that time - 1934. My Dad was Sunday School Superintendent, Training Union something I'm sure, a Deacon, on the "Pulpit" Committee, as it was called then. My Mother taught the TEL class for years and was the church librarian for a lot of years prior to her death in 1982.

I was saved in Vacation Bible School in June 1945 and was baptized by Dr. Jack McGorman.

George and I met when we were in the Young People's Department. I remember groups of us would go to other parts of Austin and serve refreshments and tell others about the Lord. We did a lot of mission activities with children. Hyde Park has always been mission minded.

In GA's we would make tray favors for the food trays in the hospitals. (That's probably not allowed today!)

George and I married at Hyde Park in 1955 with Dr. Lory Hildreth officiating. We raised our son and our daughter in the church and they both were baptized at Hyde Park.

Later, George and I worked in Sunday School with 2 year olds for a number of years then later switched to be with Adults. George also taught ESL to internationals on Sunday nights for a few years.

Hyde Park has always been a big part of my life and I love it!

Sally Jo (Bowmer) Brown

My Beginning years at Hyde Park Baptist Church.

I have long thought I should put down testimony of the grace of God I found in Hyde Park Baptist Church from a very young age. WMU organizations had a large part in my Christian growth.

It began when I was very young. I was in Sunbeams and Mrs. Bolton was the leader. Brother Tatum was the pastor, and we had a revival in the early fall. I do not remember the name of the speaker at the revival, but I do remember that I realized, at the age of 5, that I was a sinner and needed the Lord. I cried. I think the verse that broke my heart was Isaiah 53:6. Every time I heard a sermon after that I was convicted by the truth. "All we like sheep have gone astray; we have turned every one to his own way, and the Lord hath laid on Him the iniquity of us all."

I recognized that I always wanted my own way, that I would manipulate until I got my own way, and that I was in need of saving, like the sheep that wanders. More important, The God of all creation came to earth, suffered, and gave His life for me.

The next Sunday I was baptized. Is that too young? In my case it was the grace of God, because whenever doubts arose, I remembered the commitment in my heart at that time.

A few Sundays after that was the celebration of the Lord's Supper. My friend and I were not sitting with our mothers, but I wanted to participate in communion and felt qualified. A lady nearby shook her head at me and prevented me. Evil entered my heart then and I was very angry and it was many years before God got it through my head that she loved me. She just didn't know my heart. This has taught me that I must not hold grudges. It was a painful time for me, and I know now she loved me all the time.

Later we had an interim pastor, John Mills, who was a missionary in Africa. He asked for commitments to full time missionary service. God seem to speak to my heart and I went down to the front, and did so. Many times as I grew was tempted in many ways to do otherwise. God, in His grace, always brought me back to my commitment.

My mother, Ethel Bowmer, was always involved in WMU and at one time was leader of her circle. When I got older, Girls Auxiliary was a natural step. To this day I recognize verses we had to learn for our "steps," and try to quote them as I come upon them. Pauline Baldwin, Hazel Tew, and many other godly women spent time with us girls, teaching us about Salvation, the Bible, and Missions. I wish I could remember the name of the patient lady who had us for a slumber party and let us play, "Rock Around the Clock," every hour, on the hour, all night long. They took us to Belton to the annual 'House Party" there. It was there that I learned the pain that dishonesty causes. I had one extra dollar for spending money, and I left it in my room with my wallet on my bed and it was taken. This theft at a Christian event broke my heart. My friends took up a collection to replace it, but I cried because my faith in people was broken. I think this, too, was God's loving way of teaching me to let go of material things. While on the mission field in Canada, we were often broken into and things were taken, and my heart never grieved for these things. I had learned God will provide, and He always did.

When I was about eleven, there was a weekend retreat in Georgetown. I remember the college boys fighting with water guns, and wished one would notice me, but none did. I learned many years later when I met

Fred Brown that he had been at that retreat and it was a time when God was getting him back into church. I remember singing "Turn your eyes upon Jesus" and was convicted that I should be focusing on Him.

Brother Lori Hildreth was our pastor for many years, and it was he who challenged families to have "family alters," and individuals to read the Bible through. He gave us a program to start at Genesis, Psalms, and Matthew, reading a chapter in each daily and, therefore, finishing in a year. Mother and I started doing this, reading aloud to each other. This not only helped me to learn that the Bible is not many books, but one, which teaches about our sin and Savior throughout. It also helped me to learn to read well.

One important time, many years later, by this time, Dr. Ralph Smith, was there, I was walking to an evening event and noticed the sky was beautiful. God reminded me of the word to that beautiful hymn, The Love of God, especially the last verse, "Could we with ink the ocean fill and were the skies of parchment made, were every stalk on earth a quill and every man a scribe by trade, To write the love of God above would drain the ocean dry, Nor could the scroll contain the whole though stretched from sky to sky." I had again been considering staying in Texas when I graduated from nursing school, but God's love made me see I had committed to Him and would regret that old sin of self-centeredness. I thought of Paul's comment in 2 Corinthians 5:14 "For the love of Christ constraineth us, because we thus judge that, if one died for all, then were all dead."

I'm sure GA and YWA had a big part in teaching us missions in action too. The young people of Hyde Park had a Friday night mission. I remember Ann Baldwin seemed to be one of the leaders. Every Friday night we met at the church and drove to Ladesma and held a little "Sunday school" for all the children we could gather up. This ministry was eventually taken over by the Austin Baptist Association and a church was formed. We met a young man who had become a Child Evangelism worker in south Texas who was the son of that pastor.

Ann Baldwin became Ann Moore and led us in YWA later. She and her mother had always been an influence for Christ in my life. While in YWA, I was able once to go with another young lady to Glorieta and it was indeed glorious.

While I was in Brackenridge Hospital School of Nursing, one of the housemothers was a lady from Hyde Park and active in WMU. Mrs. McNeilly started a Bible study for the students and taught us about the "red ribbon of the gospel" which runs through the whole Bible to Revelation.

There was also a time when I realized I was not fit to be a missionary, that leading people to the Lord was not a thing at which I had been successful. I heard and clung to the verse in 1 Thessalonians 5:24 "Faithful is He that calleth you, who also will do it."

Still, I tried to give God conditions on which I would fully obey. I prayed for a godly mate. I was willing to go to any mission field, but I wanted a husband. I knew he had called me to nursing, and provided for my education. This longing in my heart was selfish and I knew it, but God never wants to be second place in our lives. He put us first, before himself. Finally, I committed myself to Him. To my shame, I quote that I prayed, "Even if I have to go alone." God must have chuckled, because He led me to one I least suspected. Together He has led Fred Brown and I to work among the Native people of British Columbia, Canada for 45 years. Hyde Park helped support us for most of those years. The ministry has been slow, but we have never doubted He was with us, and working through us.

Praise His Holy name, and thank you for this opportunity to share.

Peggy Miller

On August 18, 1925, a baby girl was born and given the name Peggy Alice Brooks. Her family was members of Hyde Park Baptist Church on the corner of 39th & Speedway in Austin, Texas. As an infant, Peggy was enrolled in Sunday School Cradle Roll. Then at 4 years of age, she was enrolled in Sunbeams, beginning her life study of missions. At 6 years of age, went into GA's (Girls Auxiliary) learning about and doing missions, meeting real missionaries home on furlough and listening to their mission stories.

While in GA's, at the age of 12, Peggy said she felt God calling her to be a missionary to Nigeria, Africa. When discussing this with the other girls, they said, "You can't be a missionary." This surprised her and she asked, "Why not?" They answered, "Because you can't run!" Peggy replied, "I can run—maybe not as fast as you can—but I can still run!" Going back to July 4, 1930, I had polio. It was a light case and the next year I walked from Baker Elementary School seven blocks to home, climbed up and down the steps of the 3-story school building every day! Since I participated in all the school activities, no one noticed I had had polio.

At sixteen years of age, in YWA's (Young Women's Auxiliary) I went on many trips to Mary Hardin Baylor to summer missionary camps. Many foreign missionaries were here for the summer missionary camps telling many stories of their experiences in the foreign countries. This always spurred my desire to go as a missionary.

When we married, I was automatically promoted to the WMU, (Woman's Missionary Union) and into a Circle. I have spent many years as circle chairman, program chairman, and many offices. On many Wednesday nights I spent the hour after prayer meeting helping the GA's learn their "Forward Steps" for "Mission Adventures," which is lots of scripture memorization.

I was elected as president of Hyde Park's WMU when my first son was 10 months old. The state convention was in Houston, did not have child care, so Albert, my husband, took a week's vacation to keep Bill at the hotel while I went to the convention. Before the end of my second year in office, the convention was in Corpus Christi and two weeks afterward our second son, James, was born. Two years later our third son was born. James and his two brothers were all in RA's (Royal Ambassadors), and James was the first boy at Hyde Park to be awarded the Belt for the Badges. I made sure they all attended the camps at Highland Lakes Baptist Encampment where they heard missionaries speak.

All my early years in WMU I drove all over the Hyde Park area to pick up the ladies who did not drive so they could attend the meetings. Ever since my first days in WMU, I have held an office—and still do! We have always and still meet the first Tuesday of the month for lunch and to hear missionary reports and to pray for the missionaries who have their birthday on that day. Also, we have a mission action each month to give to a local mission, and we give to the Lottie Moon Offering, Annie Armstrong Offering, and Mary Hill Davis Offering.

I also worked with Bob Ed Shotwell and Dr. Ralph Smith in the church office as Financial Secretary for 27 years. Then, when Dan Gardner became the Financial Officer, for the next seven years I was the only secretary and office Manager; all this without the help of typewriters or computers!

I am sold on all mission activities of the church wherever I can help.

As of today, I am the longest attendee of Hyde Park Baptist Church having never moved or left the area for any reason!

Pastor Kwok-Sing Cheung
Chinese Mission
HPBC
Twenty-first century missionaries

I became a Christian in 1963 while I was in college. I felt that God had called me to be a missionary to China but had not seen a clear opened door. In the sixties, China was tightly closed to the gospel. In the eighties, while I was a professor in the medical school of the University of Maryland in Baltimore, I met the first wave of scholars from China sent by the government after the Cultural Revolution. These scholars were tightly watched by the Chinese government and were not free to contact Christians to discuss spiritual matters. In the nineties, China was more opened to the West and a new wave of students and scholars came to the US. At the turn of the century, I came to Austin and became a Baptist pastor. I had the opportunities to minister to the scholars and their families from China in UT with various outreach programs in the church. I also had the opportunities to go to China on several short mission trips and found that the people in China as well as those coming to us from China were amazingly receptive to the Gospel.

God had also opened doors for me to minister to the illegal immigrants from China in a detention center near Austin in 2011. Since the inception of the program two years ago, we have more than 150 people made decision for Christ.

The rapid advancement of air transportation and the globalization of every facet of society have brought people together from every part of the world previously thought impossible. In the twenty-first century, if God calls one to serve Him as a foreign missionary, one can serve Him in the home turf without traveling to a foreign country. I believe God has prepared me for a ministry such as this.

Look at all the caps Mineola Grumbles knitted!

Pastor Cheung in the Orange and White Cap with Seminary Class.

The class is posing in church wearing Mineola's hats.

Nancy Arista
Austin, Texas
September 15, 2013
MY MISSION EXPERIENCE

Thanks to the Lottie Moon Offering, Southern Baptist missionaries began their work in Lima, Peru in 1950. My parents, my little brother, and I began attending Primera Iglesia Bautista (First Baptist Church) when I was 4 years old in 1956. Although I do not recall this, my late Mom told me I participated in the sunbeams program.

My earliest recollection of my mission's involvement was with the Auxiliar de Niñas (Girls Auxiliary) as a teenager. Our leader encouraged us to achieve all the "steps" of this program. Each step required Bible verses memorization, studying about missionaries' lives, performing mission action projects, among other activities. I diligently pursued each step. I became a Princess, Queen, Queen Regent, and Queen with Scepter. When I reached the top in 1968, we met on a Saturday night at church. I prepared a speech concerning my personal experiences and read it to the congregation. Several girls were being recognized. All Queens wore long white dresses. It was such an important event for the church members, who like my parents, were very supportive. I can visualize how adults had their Sunday attire on: ladies wore dresses and men had their suits and ties on. After the recognition service, we had a reception, and the church members congratulated us individually. Yes, it was a meaningful night!

 I was particularly delighted that we had the CREAM OF THE CROP when I served in this ministry. It was spectacular to watch the young ladies grow spiritually through the years. The leaders and I took groups to Germany for a camp with 3rd through 6th grade girls in 1991. We went to Burbank, CA in about 1992 to lead a Vacation Bible School. In 1994 we went to Caracas, Venezuela for another VBS. Acteen work is not an easy program. Despite having to work on their multiple tasks for each step, the girls also had to plan ALL the activities for each domestic and international event. We also raised funds: girls and leaders cleaned the church parking lot, cooked pancakes for breakfast one Sunday at Hyde Park, gathered recipes for a cookbook, assembled those cookbooks and sold them, and had garage sales, among other projects... And this is a small sample of my mission's involvement, and it is not over... Heading to Sendai, Japan in a few days to minister to folks who suffered losses due to the 2011 tsunami.

Rachel Frey

Mark 13:10 "And the gospel must first be published among all nations."

At a very young age, I heard many preachers speak that the world needed Jesus and it set my heart to thinking of seeing those around the world know of Jesus. At the time I did not know the word "missions or missionary."

When I was about 13, I was introduced to GAs. The teacher had a great interest, not only of our learning more of the Bible, but included stories of missionaries and the gospel being preached and taught around the world. She encouraged us each to receive the mission magazine each month. From that, I developed a love for writing to the missionaries and praying for them. At one time in my early twenties I felt the call to go as a missionary, but due to some extenuating circumstances, I was not elected.

Later on, I married a minister and taught him to love missions also. We were able to lead the churches he pastored to support missions liberally. We had missionaries from Brazil, Bolivia, Taiwan, the Philippines, Portugal, and Mexico in our home, some for extended periods of time. I never tired of the stories of reaching people of foreign lands for the Lord. We were able to go on several short-term mission trips and serve in teaching and medical missions.

WMU and its organizations have been a central part in my church work throughout my life. I have served in various offices, but mostly taught Sunbeams. It is my prayer that I was able to teach many children to love God's Word and missionaries that carry that Word to all nations

Ruth Ruiz
MY MISSION STORY

After visiting several churches in my community, I chose to become a Baptist at the age of 14. I enjoyed every new adventure there, teaching 3 year olds along with a saintly lady, Sra. Vargas, now in heaven. I grew quickly in Training Union, where all young people came together to learn and share the mission stories we had studied. When Missionaries came to our meetings, I encouraged others to get an autograph and we later studied their whereabouts. This was a wonderful time to be in the Young Peoples Department. Four years later, I was director of the GA's (Girl's Auxiliary, a part of Women Mission Union). My job was to teach the 19 teenager girls the steps to graduation and eventually the coronation—a big to-do. My favorite adventure was teaching 12 year olds in Sunday School. They had quite an imagination, mountains of energy, and kept me studying from 3-4 bibles during the week before Sunday morning.

In 1972, I joined Hyde Park Baptist Church. I immediately came to WMU where I was embraced by great, strong Christian women like Belle Froelich, Peggy Miller, Dora Roberts, Pauline Baldwin, Vera Menn, Mrs. McNeilly, (the same Mrs. McNeilly who was the housemother at Brackenridge School of Nursing) who introduced me to The Baptist Community Center, where I have served many years. Other great WMU women whom God placed in my path were Hazel Tew, (who loved books and shared with me great writers of the faith), and of course Bob Ed Shotwell, who later was President of WMU. This list could go on, but there were so many saints that placed their hands over mine and led me though our beautiful faith and Bible

Hyde Park families are always "On Mission for God." My mission field today is the Church Library, where for the past 15 years we have guided teachers, and so many others, to seek out our valuable collection of fiction and non-fiction materials. It is a joy to hand over a book by Christian writers such as Wiersbe, Graham, Lotz, Lucado, Charles Spurgeon, Matthew Henry and so many others that will aid in the growth of new Christians. Often teachers will stop by the Library and ask for quick information on "Solomon's Temple," or "what happened to each Disciple," or "what does our faith say about etc., etc.." Our Mission is to get the best Christian and Baptist materials in their hands .We all need inspiration to lead lives that honor God. We must remember the great men and women of the past who can inspire us to renewed purpose. We have a mission going on right here at Hyde Park Baptist Church, and we're so fortunate to have this extension of our faith and church and that I have a small part in it.

Daphne Hodges, Missionary of the week
January 24, 2004

Daphne Hodges loves to see people learn. As a public school speech pathologist, she was blessed to see children overcoming barriers and becoming successful. Though she no longer serves in that role, the blessings of seeing lives changed continues in her work as site coordinator for the Christian Women's Job Corps (CWJC) at Hyde Pak Baptist Church in Austin, TX. Since beginning in Spring 2001, she has seen many ladies graduate from a life of uncertainty to one of hope and promise.

Her work with CWJC started with a prayer card three years ago. On the card was a picture of Chris Rowley, a former CWJC site coordinator at another Austin church. "I had been looking for the place God could use me, but had not been satisfied with any place I had served," said Daphne. "I visited with Chris, who told me she had been praying for someone to become coordinator and start a group at Hyde Park."

Daphne retired from teaching and began preparing for the new ministry. "And I've been busy ever since," she said.

Keeping her busy are ladies seeking love, acceptance, and "just someone to believe in them." After 8-10 weeks in the program, tangible results are obvious. They find Christ, learn new skills, and begin believing in themselves.

Pray for this work to continue to be a witness to all. Pray for more commitment of mentors for the ladies.

Chris Rowley and a new graduate of CWJC, JULY 2002

In addition to serving as site coordinator for Christian Women' Job Corps, Daphne worked in the evening childcare program from 1996 until 2012, serving as Childcare director from 1998-2001.

In the spring of 2004, Daphne began teaching in the Hyde Park Preschool program. For the past ten years she has taught four and five year olds. Daphne also taught a senior adult ladies Sunday School class since 2003.

For several years, Daphne has worked closely with the Senior Adult minister coordinating trips, Bible Studies and various other activities for senior adults and has organized several women's seminar events. At present, Daphne is working with the managers of a large apartment complex in preparation to starting a women's ministry program and summer Bible study program at that site.

Bee Klingemann

Growing through Missions

It was through the memorization of the scriptures about salvation in the GA "Forward Steps" during the 1950s that I came to know Jesus as my Savior. My mother, as WMU president in our little country church, went to extraordinary lengths to make sure my sister and our friends and I had the opportunity to be involved in Girls Auxiliary. Though our young GA leadership fizzled after a year or two, Mama kept me interested in learning and doing the missions steps until she was able to take me each week to Congress Avenue Baptist Church, which at that time had strong missions education programs for all ages. Enthusiastic GA and YWA counselors were there to encourage me through my high school years.

My parents also became very involved with international students attending the University of Texas. These students were often in our home where they received a strong witness and became our very good friends. A few years later, "Friendship" began as a way of ministering to the needs of international women in Austin, most of whose husbands were UT students. My mother was one of the founding Baptist women of Friendship and served in childcare and sewing for the first two years. As a mom with two small children, and not yet driving, I was not quite ready for the Friendship experience. (For a number of years, Baptist ladies would visit their assigned friends before the first Friendship day in the fall and provide transportation for them both ways each Thursday.) When my mother became ill, I devoted more and more time to caring for her with my two little ones in tow. Mama continued to stay in touch with her international friends and prayed earnestly for them. The year of her death, I began driving, and Friendship was at the top of my list of new activities. The first time I went to a large apartment complex to invite an international lady to Friendship, there came a heavy rain such that I was unable to see numbers on the buildings, nor could I see where I was driving. My big car ended up on a concrete drain cover with no traction to get off it! Just as I was trying to decide what to do (no cell phone of course) God sent one of his angels with a winch. This kind man did his magic with the winch and I was on my way home with my little girls to return and try again another day. In the years I was in Friendship, I had friends from Indonesia, Japan, two from Mexico, and Iran. Four of those came to know Jesus through Friendship. Another friend was from Austria, and already a strong believer in Christ. She and her husband, an American, were working towards appointment by the IMB. They have served in Jordan, Sudan, and now France. Many stories could be told about those relationships.

Eventually, God led in some other directions, including Sunday School leadership for preschoolers, GAs, Mission Friends, and curriculum writing for both Sunday School and WMU (Mission Friends). Once, while filling out a questionnaire to write for GAs, a question about participation in mission trips stopped me. This was something I had long wanted to do, so I began praying for an affordable opportunity to go on a yearly mission trip. Our WMU decided to sponsor a family mission trip to Ciudad Juarez. Soon I was helping to organize this venture, not once, but several years in a row. Eventually, violence in that city prevented us from taking groups there. But our love for the Hands of Luke Medical Ministries was and is such that Henry and I have continued to go each year to help with special holiday outreaches extending from El Paso to Cd. Juarez. Missions have been a key component in all these activities and more.

We still see many opportunities for mission involvement here at home and beyond. We pray for God's continued leadership in discovering His "when, where, and how" for us.

J. Henry Klingemann
My Missions Story

A message by my pastor, Charles Stewart, when I was nine years old —a message about serving Christ and others—sparked a desire in me that led to my accepting Christ as my Savior and a lifetime of serving Him in missions and ministry endeavors.

Not long after my decision to follow Jesus, a family friend, Olen Miles, invited me, my brothers, and our cousins to help prepare the ground on which Highland Lakes Baptist Encampment would be built. Our assignment was picking up rocks all over that acreage! We may not have understood the great role the camp would have in the salvation of souls, but we were among the first to share in that mission. Besides having many good memories at Highland lakes as a teenager, I have had the opportunity to take many boys to camp there, and seen some of them receive Christ there.

Soon after my wife and I married, we joined Hillcrest Baptist Church. Right away the need for Royal Ambassador leadership was made known to me. Together, Bo Parker and I answered that call and served together for 14 years. Across 49 years of RA leadership in four local churches, I have had the joy of introducing many boys to real participation in missions and have witnessed the salvation and growth in Christ-likeness of many. Some of these Ambassadors for Christ have even become RA leaders themselves.

We came to Hyde Park Baptist Church in December 1990, and I continued working with RAs under the excellent leadership of James Nelson. The following year, I found myself directing RAs once again. In addition, opportunities came to serve at the associational level which led to years of involvement at the state level of RA leadership, part of the Texas Baptist Men's ministries. Currently, I serve as a regional RA Trainer and TBM Advocate, treasurer for our Austin Baptist Association Disaster Relief Team --also a ministry of TBM-- and a board member for Highland Lakes Camp and Conference Center.

Some years ago, my wife and I were able to provide some leadership for family mission trips to Ciudad Juarez, in Mexico, inspired by the amazing work of the Hands-of-Luke Medical Ministries, and sponsored by our Hyde Park WMU. A few years of summertime Vacation Bible Schools, construction, and prison visits gave way to helping provide Thanksgiving meals, along with a live gospel witness, to many thousands of impoverished people in Juarez and El Paso for several years. All along, we were and have continued collecting new socks and underwear, toys and other items to be given to several thousand children each year in the Colonias of Juarez. In the past few years, we have added colorful gospel tracts for kids, written in Spanish, to include with the other gifts. Hyde Park people have been very generous with their money, which has enhanced our church's ability to make a significant contribution to "Regalos de Amor" (Gifts of Love). We always look forward to December, and filling the Christmas bags for the children.

All of these missions endeavors, and more on a personal level, have been an adventure in following Christ and serving Him as an Ambassador for Christ.

Adults: Joyce Parker, Coordinator of Women on Mission,
Henry Klingemann, Director of Royal Ambassadors,
Dora Roberts, Director, Women's Missionary Union
RA's: Nathan Newell, Ron Trail, and Mikey Newell

DR. BAXTER & MRS. WANDA WOMACK
Dictated to Julia Petter

Dr. Baxter & Wanda Womack arrived in 1961 at HPBC. The Womack family has attended Hyde Park and raised their children here since their arrival. Mrs. Wanda did so until she answered her call home to the Lord in February of 2012. Dr. Womack is still a member and attends regularly.

Baxter became an active member of the Deacon body at HPBC, which was primarily considered a "Blue collar," church and set in a very undesirable neighborhood. It was surrounded by University students and housing that catered to the students. Dr. Ralph Smith was the Pastor at that time and along with the Church, the Building Committee, the Missions Committee, the WMU and the Deacon body strategically went about purchasing lots and property in the neighborhood in order to 'upgrade,' the neighborhood. Mrs. Wanda served on the Building Committee a good many years and her desire to improve the church and its reputation were clearly evident throughout her time of service.

Eleven of pieces of property were purchased around Hyde Park and the Building Committee went about transforming the neighborhood into what it is today. Mrs. Wanda worked full time but still found time after retirement to attend the WMU Luncheons and stay quite active in church.

Baxter was Missions Committee Chair for about 14 years and saw the neighborhood grow and become better. He is an ardent supporter of the Acteens organization and WMU Missions as they have evolved thru the years. Although Dr. Womack has not ever 'traveled' on Mission; he does Missions daily, living by the code of sharing **John 3:16** wherever and whenever he has the opportunity; from the grocery clerk to waiters and waitresses at any restaurant he may visit.

Dr. Womack says that he does not worry about the WMU organization, as it has always seemed to be in good hands. It has worked alongside the other organizations of the church to help maintain their success.

EDITORS NOTE: Dr. Baxter Womack, retired Professor of Electrical Engineering, University of Texas, commented that Hyde Park was an undesirable neighborhood. This may have been true in his opinion, but it was a perfect place to minister to the hippies and university students. The HP neighborhood was named for HYDE PARK, in England, an exclusive subdivision, and in the beginning had very expensive homes with very influential residents. The Austin Street Car ran from downtown to Hyde Park and back, but not to any other part of town. In the 1960's the university enrollment boomed and the students populated many neighborhoods around campus. Hyde Park is still an expensive, prosperous part of Austin, Texas.

Peter Tadin

I am humbled to have been asked what my mission's story at Hyde Park is, as I know there are so many other faithful servants at my church whom I've looked up to for many years who have their own story to tell. However, my story began in January of 1986 when I first visited Hyde Park and have been very involved in the singles ministry ever since. I learned that Pastor Dr. Ralph Smith was starting churches here in Austin and that got me excited. Back in the late 80's and '90's, the singles ministry was spearheaded by John Walters, who was the singles minister on staff at Hyde Park. I viewed him not only as a friend, but as a visionary and enabler of Christian singles to feel connected and get involved in the church. In working with John, I approached him early on with the idea of doing singles mission trips to expand the scope of the ministry into outreach missions and give singles some hands-on experience that could help them grow spiritually. Our first singles mission trip was to Saltillo, Mexico, where we taught Bible studies and helped do construction on a church. After that, the ball was rolling and we followed that up with several yearly mission trips to very small Baptist churches in Colorado and in West Virginia. Working side-by-side with local bi-vocational pastors in reaching out to their local communities was exciting and spiritually rewarding as we touched people's lives in the name of Jesus. We led vacation bible schools and sports camps, which allowed us to reach children of all ages. One of the most rewarding experiences was when we were doing a door-to-door visitation outreach in the tiny community of Kremmling, Colorado. God used Carol Lee and me to share Christ with a woman who was surprised at our visit but opened up to us like old friends. She accepted Christ before we left.

In the 2000's, we did a couple of mission trips to Poland to work alongside Baptist missionary, Jerry Goss, in reaching out to the Roma People (Gypsies), a highly discriminated group in Europe. My fondest memory of working with these people was having the privilege of not only teaching Jesus to their children but also having them call me their friend, which is highly usual for them to call someone that who is on the outside. In 2009, I went with Pastor Cheung, pastor of Hyde Park's Chinese congregation, on a mission trip to Taiwan to work with the aboriginal Taiwanese and Chinese children. This was a very rewarding experience in being used by God to lead several of them to the Lord and to see them baptized in front of their parents in a country where only 3% are considered Christian. It was also exciting to return to Taiwan on a mission trip, after having served there as a summer missionary in 1980 when I was in college 29 years before.

In January 2010, a small group of singles made up of Robert Horan, Josh Williams, Eric Dooley, and I headed over to Romania on a mission trip with Pastor Samuel Clintoc who was the Romanian Pastor at Hyde Park at the time. We reached out to the poorer Romanians to pray with them and give them a sack of groceries. Their eyes would light up like a dear friend had showed up on their doorstep to bless them. It was truly sharing Christ by giving them a loaf of bread but also telling them about the Bread of Life.

Of course, I also participated in, led, and assisted with many local mission opportunities here in the Austin area such as the Austin Baptist Chapel Soup Kitchen in east Austin, Widows Work Days, delivering fruit baskets to homebounds at Christmas, working with the children at the Texas Baptist Children's Home in Round Rock, street evangelism on 6th Street downtown, hospital visitation, leading Bible studies, doing nursing home outreaches, participating in a rake-and-bake with our Hyde Park neighbors, and doing Monday night visitation of those who recently visited Hyde Park. Many of these ministries I continue to work at to this day. I am also excited about how Pastor Kie Bowman, whom I see as a visionary, is starting churches, too, or should I just say, expanding Hyde Park in unique ways to reach out to today's communities here in Austin where the fields are ripe unto the harvest.

As I mentioned earlier, there are many others at Hyde Park who have their own missions' story to tell, many of whom are spiritual giants who work away from the spotlight, but yet their work is felt by everyone. This only serves as a testament that Hyde Park is truly a missions' church that God uses to shine His light not only in Austin, but also around the world through its people.

Verna L. Warwick
God's Beautiful Plan for Missions

Step by step, God unfolds His beautiful plan, like the petals of an opening flower. After each petal opens, you can begin to see some of beauty He had in mind.

I was sitting in my easy chair wearing a body brace after major back surgery. It was one of the darkest times of my life! The surgery had involved the removal of my lower rib to do a bone fusion between the thoracic eleventh and twelfth vertebra. I suffered much pain in the back and left lung, which had been drained during the surgery. Little did I know, I was in training for what God was about to do! Day by day, I spent my time studying the word. The more I studied, the more God spoke to my heart! I began to read places in the word, which speak of the people in darkness. "The way of the wicked is darkness." (Proverbs 4:19) I thought of all the many people across the world, which dwells in darkness. Through scripture, God touched my heart with concern for those lost and in darkness. The Lord spoke to my heart about going somewhere across seas for mission service. I did not know where or how, but I knew God was calling me for this!

Later I spoke to my husband, Charles, about my experience. He said God had not spoken to him about this. The idea was tabled for a while. I still had much recovery to do as well. One day, Charles came to me and said, "Now, I know we are supposed to go somewhere special for the Lord!"

Our first inquiry was to the Home Mission Board, which sends people both home and abroad. There was an open door for China, but there were applicants more educated than ourselves. Not long afterward, we had a call from Dale Gore of the Austin Baptist Association. I heard him say, "Verna, I want you and Charles to pray about going to Brazil with Partnership Missions." Those petals were unfolding. God had opened a brand new door we had never thought of! God works in mysterious ways! Our open door was Curitiba, Brazil. God's hand was clearly evident. The door for China closed, but the Lord had opened another door!

Once in Curitiba, we began to see many ministry needs. There was a park in the area of our Mission Vida Nova, meaning "New Life" in Portuguese. We were able to bring Bible Stories to kids who came there to play. There was much freedom to go into the schools there. We were able to take puppet shows into public schools. Charles was even able to speak and bring the plan of salvation in one of the schools, something we could not do at home. We were treated as celebrities in one junior high school, where students begged for our autographs. I wanted them to know we were not celebrities, but represented the King of the Universe!

Revival was going on in evenings at our Mission. We spoke through interpreters, Pastor Alex and others. Cindy Klingemann and I took the children to a small room during services where we told them Bible stories with an interpreter. I had brought teaching supplies and pictures in a separate suitcase. When we left Brazil, I donated the supplies, since they had none to speak of. At the end of the stay, we were driven to the site of the brand new Mission under construction. We began to understand how Partnership Missions works, when we ran into another mission team in Florida airport on our return to the states. A team of builders follows an evangelistic team, according to God's plan. Some plant, some water, but God gives the increase! Glory!

Elizabeth Harris
My WMU Story

"I am a Sunbeam, I am a Sunbeam…" or I was a Sunbeam and now my daughters are Mission Friends. The three decades in between those times have been a great adventure on mission with God.

I grew up in a Southern Baptist church and loved being a part of the mission's programs. My mother went through the programs to the crowning stage! When I was in elementary school, we moved to a smaller town and smaller church without children's mission programs. But in that church, I did a presentation to the whole church on who Annie Armstrong was, and why it is important to give to missions. Also, at preteen camp, I felt the call to foreign missions. God didn't tell me I would live in a village in Africa but kept the call wide open, which looking back now is good, because I have been blessed to be a part of many different types of service.

I began my missionary journey by painting a church in San Antonio. Then we traveled to Mexico, for more painting and partnering with a local church.

In college I was part of the BSM, did Beach Reach one spring break, as well as a few other USA mission trips. I fell in love with a friend while he was on a GoNow Mission project to Australia; we wrote letters! I then did a summer trip teaching English in refugee camps and playing basketball with a Palestinian team.

We got married and took part of the ISC opportunity to spend two years with a team overseas.

We came back and began to reach internationals living here in Texas. I love speaking to groups to share what God is doing around the world and how we are all called to be a part, including my daughters' Mission Friends group. We spent time leading and participating in trips with our church: distribution in London, family mission trip and youth World Changers-I was back to painting in Jesus' name.

Through it all, I have learned a lot. I have learned that the support of the church, including WMU, is vital. I have learned that God values everything done in his name and because of his love. Each Bible given to one who had never had one is important; each act of love shown to the 'least of these' in important; each encouragement of a child to be a missionary is important; each ESL lesson is important. We are all His hands and feet!

John & Priscilla White
Christmas 2013

Priscilla White
Mission Story

When I was just a young Christian, I read about missionaries and developed a great love and admiration for the selfless lives they lived. Their commitment and love for obeying God's commandment to "GO AND TELL" rooted itself in my soul! I prayed that God would use me in this way. Then life happened and though I married and had a family, I never ceased to have a love for serving where God led me. The doors to full time service never opened for John and me. So my plan of being a full-time missionary was not the same as God's plan for me. From time to time I pondered the situation with disappointment until John said that being in the military and traveling around the world we could still bring God's message. We would be self-supported missionaries. This worked out perfectly and we thank God for the direction He has led us. There is no way my story can equal the Christians who have given their lives in faraway places and suffered great hardships and never quit striving for the Lord! But it is a story of love—God's love through me to a lost world. I pray it will encourage you and set a fire burning within you that leads you to total commitment and service to spread the Gospel to a lost world wherever God leads you! "You can do all things through Christ who strengthens you!"

We started out in Okinawa, Japan. The children were very active in the youth group and our church, (Koza Baptist Church), was busy reaching out to the Okinawan community. There were some Christian churches there and we painted them and assisted in various ways to share the gospel with the local folks. We met a Doctor from Canada who was living on Okinawa teaching medicine to the Okinawan doctors. His wife, Margaret, had English classes for their wives and friends using the Bible. They were self-supported missionaries and great ambassadors for the Lord! We became fast friends. Christopher asked John to go to Borneo on a mission trip with him and the following year he asked both of us to go into the jungle for a couple of weeks. I must admit that I was more than a little bit terrified. I am a city girl and can't stand dirt and bugs and have a stomach that is particular. Food is my Achilles heel! If it doesn't look good and smell good, it may get swallowed down but it is coming back up, and that could be embarrassing and hinder the Lord's work. So after hearing about the fungus and "stuff" that John had eaten on his previous trip, I spent many hours in prayer wrestling with my human weaknesses. Finally, I said I would go but began to write my farewell notes for my children and family, because I was convinced I would not come back alive. Nevertheless, I knew God wanted me to go so I had to be obedient, live or die. This was before the time of cell phones, computers, iPads, etc.. They didn't even have electricity or any form of civilized life we were used to in the jungle. The arrangements were set up six months in advance and we knew basically what tribes and villages we would visit and were studying and preparing our lessons.

We left Okinawa and our three children in the midst of a Typhoon and flew to Taipei and from there to Hong Kong. We met Christopher's sister, Francis, and spent the night with her and flew on the next day to Borneo. We stopped at Brunei and were surrounded by guards with machine guns. We did not have to get off the plane and added a few passengers and flew on to Kota Kinabalu. We met many of Christopher and Margaret's friends, and the Christian community was small and struggling amidst the Moslem population. Even back then, the Moslems hated the Christians and showed it. The people there were very big on shaking hands so much so that my whole arm was aching by the end of the day. Two Christian ladies were on vacation and had allowed us to use their cold water flat there. The little church group met in Mr. Pang's house. He had a little tub for baptisms and grew a garden amidst the chairs scattered around for the meetings. That night the Moslems threw rocks at us and they sometimes broke through the corrugated roof, but no one was hurt. Sometimes we had to have three or more translators depending on who attended the meetings. We set off the next morning for the interior and mile 6. Places were not identified so much by name as by the mile markers. There was a fair road built in the middle of the jungle by the Australians during the Second World War. It began and ended in the jungle.

It was quite like the old Tarzan movies without Tarzan! It was beautiful, with orchids growing in the trees and flowers everywhere, deadly, and hot, humid, and steamy. There was no air conditioning or cooling since we left Hong Kong. Nor did we have clear cool drinking water outside of Sandakan and our apartment. I had secreted away 6 breakfast bars for survival in the bottom of my pack. We carried our clothes, medications for malaria, sleeping gear, Bibles and bug spray. There was no place to buy anything. We spent our first night in Kadazan Village with a family that had no children so they bought one from a family who had too many, a common practice then. Christopher and Margaret had lived in Borneo for many years, and there were Christians spread about the villages and tribes as a result of their work.

We lived among the natives. We traveled down the brown rivers staying at different villages teaching and preaching. Most of the time we were well received. We ate what they ate and drank muddy brown warm water. That's what we brushed our teeth in and bathed in. Sometimes the only water for a bath came from dipping an old rusty can into a brown mud hole and pouring it over you. We lived in the huts, slept on bamboo floors without privacy and basic civilized facilities. We were treated well by the tribes, respected, and a source of great curiosity. This was good, because the people came from everywhere to hear the preaching and they would not start until they sang. Wow! They could really sing! There was a great love for the Lord. They hungered for the word and would sit for hours in the heat and sometimes on the ground or logs and benches with no complaint. The children were quick to learn and memorized their verses. They were like children anywhere. They played and were into everything. They had no houses like ours, just bamboo huts.

Telupid   Hand cranked record player   Leaving Telupid for the interior by river

They had no material possessions to speak of but were rich in their love for God and His word. One village had Bible studies every night of the week. The meeting places were like open-air pavilions. The nurseries, if they had any, consisted of a large spring tied to a rope hung over the rafters with a sarong tied to the end. The baby was placed in the "iyongs" and the mother would bounce it up and down every once in a while. At night, you could see the little lanterns coming through the jungle trails as the folks came for the meetings. It was always packed full, and there was much commotion with animals and children moving about and folks shaking hands. People were saved and baptized. We even had a wedding.

About the time I began to feel like I might make it home alive, we visited a floating village. It was a Moslem village and some friends of the Willises lived there and we were going for a visit and for Christopher to witness to them. Our welcome was warm and friendly. The women in the family only were seen when they came out to serve the tea and bring something. After we left, a crowd gathered and began to follow us. Some asked for money and others were threatening us. I thought this might not end well and was doing a lot of praying. The hostility was growing and we were completely surrounded and unable to move toward the dirt road we had walked in on. All of a sudden the crowd of men separated a little and a taxi appeared out of nowhere and stopped for us. There was no reason for the taxi to be there. No one could call, for there were no phones. It was definitely sent by God, and it saved us from a lot of trouble. Praise God for His mercy and grace!

Back in our little flat, we enjoyed the cold shower with clean water. We enjoyed the clear water to drink. It was odd to sit in a chair and sleep in a bed again. What luxury!! We began house visits then throughout the city and every place we went, they fed us something. I often switched plates with John, who is blessed with an iron constitution and can eat anything called food. We shared the Gospel and encouraged believers along the way.

Our last afternoon we spent going out to an area where the government was trying to preserve the Orangutans. The deforestation was causing a lot of animals to die. As the sun began to go down, we could see movement in the forest. Watching, we could see the Orangutans swinging through the trees from vine to vine until they came into the clearing where we stood. Christopher asked the guide if he had any trouble with them and he responded, "No, but that only one was bad and she only bit white women." That was comforting! One came up to me and put a hand on my knee. I reached down and grabbed the hand and then another hand grabbed my knee and I took it in my other hand. Then another hand/foot grabbed my knee and I said, "John, please help!" He laughed and was busy taking pictures. Finally, the guide came and popped the little beastie on the head and I was freed. We met the Christians for dinner and had a wonderful fellowship. The food was good, but the blessing of being used by God to reach the people and share and encourage them was far better! We reached home safely and when I unpacked, I found 6 badly crushed breakfast bars. They were never opened, for God took care of every need. He provided bountifully all along the way. What a mighty God we serve!

Our latest trip into Taiwan was a great blessing. We went with members of our Chinese congregation. The flight was smooth but long. We had a 5-hour layover in Japan and arrived in Taipei about 10:00 the next night. We drove to the mission house where we spent the night. (Getting there at 11:30 and leaving at 6:00 the next morning.) We met the rest of the 80-member team at the train station and settled in for our 7-hour train ride. We were traveling light with a backpack and a small suitcase. I think we were the only "round eyes" on the trip. We were so excited to see what God was going to do at the "English" camp. How unlike that first mission trip, for we had cell phones, IPads, computers, box lunches, purified water, clean, comfortable air conditioned transportation and stores along the way. We stayed in an old spa on the side of a mountain overlooking the ocean. It was clean, adequate, and air-conditioned. We did not expect such accommodations and were thanking God for His goodness. The first morning we ate breakfast in the spa. It must have been usual stuff for the Chinese but I had to pick and choose. I settled on my favorites, cabbage and onions and some kind of green vegetable with peanuts. All fun to eat with chopsticks. They had Nutella and jelly and margarine and bread, coffee, tea and water. Some mornings, we had fried eggs. There was always something good to eat.

We met in the pavilion overlooking the ocean and had our devotions for the day followed by a brief team meeting for the classes we would do that day. We taught English using Bible stories. We started with Adam and Eve, then Noah, Abram, The Good Samaritan, The Prodigal Son, and Jesus. They were very quick to learn and I was amazed that they were not only fluent with their native language but were learning English too. Each morning we had class till noon and went back to the gym to play games and have lunch. After lunch, there was a basketball camp for those who wanted to participate, and a good many did. Some of us stayed and cheered them on. Then we went back to the spa to rest up and get ready for supper and reports and going out to visit families in the community. We found many idol worshipers and ancestor worshipers. Christianity is not forbidden, and it is considered kind of cool to be a Christian. It presents a problem when you ask someone if they are Christian, because most will say yes. Then you ask them if they still go to the mountain. If they say yes, it means they go up there to worship the white snake. They have many Gods and it is difficult to get them to renounce all other gods and serve Jehovah God alone. People would stop on the street and listen as you went through the plan of salvation. Many would pray to receive Christ and some would go home to think about it.

Our meeting hall (gym) was an oven. No air conditioners or fans but God worked His miracles there and in the classrooms and every place we went. It was wonderful to see the response from the children. When each one in our class was led through the plan of salvation, each one prayed to receive Christ; it was fantastic to see God work!! It was amazing to see souls saved and lives changed by the power of the Holy Spirit. Many of the children had committed to follow Christ, and visits were planned to talk with their parents. It is customary to wait till you are 18 to get baptized. So we visited and sent notes home. Many had prayed and were saved. We were overjoyed to see 24 baptized in the pool the next day. We went out by teams at night and made cold calls. God's word was spread all over the little village and surrounding places. How could personal discomfort matter when you are busy for the Lord! It couldn't ever be that hot or humid or dirty or whatever. When God is in control, everything will work out for His glory. It was hard to leave, but we have since heard from our leader that an evangelical church will be started there in the coming weeks. Praise God! As our leader said, "We all experienced that **impossible is I'm possible -- with GOD!**

From our first venture, God has sent us on numerous mission trips, each one special and rewarding. Each one growing my faith and strengthening my courage, knowing I could trust God for everything in every circumstance. We have been to Asia many, many times over the years, and I have a deep love for those people. The Christian community is growing so fast there and they are often undergoing persecution and hardship. God is using all of this for His glory.

His kingdom is growing and His people are growing in number and strength. We have been to Europe and seen the same lostness. This is where the Reformation began, and now the churches are almost empty. So many places we have been challenged to go to and we see the same thing, including our own country. There are fields white unto harvest and where are the laborers. The world is hungry for the "Good News" and we need committed workers who will go and tell. We need support for those who do go and tell. What are you spending your time and treasure on? Someday we will give an accounting to God for our lives and may we not be ashamed for the choices we have made.

An orangutan on Priscilla

Home away from home be it ever so humble!

John White's Mission Story

John was invited to go on a mission trip with Dr. Willis and two other people. It was the beginning of a wonderful journey and the source of joy and purpose for the rest of his life. The following is a copy of a letter that John wrote about his trip.

Greetings to all and praise God for His everlasting goodness to us. This trip to Borneo was a special blessing to me and I am truly thankful that God through Christopher gave me the opportunity to see the fields so ripe for harvest.

On August 5, we four left from Naha International Airport, (Pastor Higa, Dr. Christopher Willis, his son Chris, and I). Pastor Higa has a local church in Yonabaru. Dr. Willis is one of the most devoted servants of our Lord Jesus Christ I know. He was born in Shanghai where his father was a self-supported missionary. His Dad was an engineer by trade. Dr. Willis worked for 8 years in Malaysia as a self-supporting missionary where he built and maintained a hospital in the middle of the jungle. When the Moslems came to power, the Willis family was ordered to leave. Every year for the past 10 years Christopher has returned to Borneo for 2 weeks to encourage the believers and bring God's message again to the meetings that were established and many who'd never heard. Christopher's son, (we called Didi) is studying medicine at Chubo Hospital in Okinawa and looks like he will follow his father's footsteps.

From the beginning I knew it was going to be a wonderful trip, because the devil tried his best to ruin it. Pastor Higa had a lot of difficulty getting his visa. The first morning at the airport we were told there would be a 6-hour delay. We passed the time and when we finally got to Taipei, Pan Am cancelled our next flight and we waited for 7 hours before we got another flight to Hong Kong.

Christopher's sister, Francis, met us at the airport. Instead of arriving at 10:30 that morning, we arrived at 10:30 that night and it was nice to have supper waiting.

At 7:45 the next morning we left Kai Tak Airport for Koto Kinabalu, Malaysia arriving there at noon. The airport at Kinabalu was like walking into an old Humphrey Bogart movie, a step back in time and full of surprises. A friend of Christopher's met us at the airport. She had been in one of his Sunday school classes. Trying to get tickets to Sandakan was short of a nightmare. There were no lines only a mass of people all clamoring for service. Thanks to the experience of Dr. Willis, he was able to get our tickets.

At 14:35 we arrived in Sandakan where a large crowd had turned out to welcome Christopher. It was wonderful to see the love in each face for their dear Christian Brother. They had a caravan of cars and yours truly had to sit in the front because, "I was so big!"

Some Christian ladies who ran a dispensary in the city were on a holiday in Canada and had made their apartment available for our use while we were there. While Christopher visited his friend Mr. Pang, we left the apartment and walked around.

That night, at a meeting on Mr. Pang's rooftop, Pastor Higa and I gave our testimonies and Christopher spoke in Malaysian and English.

Sunday was a busy day as were all our days there. At morning services we had the Lord's Supper and two Baptisms. This was my first experience at passing a community cup as Jesus did at the last supper. We stayed in Sandakan 3 days and had several meetings and visits there while we prepared for our trip into the interior.

We left early Tuesday morning, August 9th by land rover to Tellupid where we stopped about noon for a dinner of rice and chicken. We had several meetings there and God blessed us wonderfully. Christopher baptized 8 in the river at Tellupid. Several times it rained and we had no meetings because it was impossible to hear with the torrent of rain falling on the tin roofs.

For breakfast we had fresh fried pineapple and really enjoyed it. Then we loaded everything into the boat and left. The boat was similar to a canoe, but made of wood. There were 12 of us, including the boatman's wife and 3 children and all of our gear packed tightly inside.

The next meetinghouse at Bulis was locked and we had to climb in the windows to open up. After Christopher spoke he checked on the sick. That was the night we ate unrecognizable fungus. One of the women held something up and asked Christopher if he would eat it. He asked her if she ate it and she said yes, so Christopher said we'd eat it too. And we did!

We were sleeping in one of the native houses built on stilts and sleeping on split bamboo floors. That night I got so cold I got up and dressed and then went back to bed. On the 13th we stopped at the Lever Brother's oil palm plantation and bought a cook stove and tea pot and other supplies to continue our trip.

One of our meetings was especially precious to me. The people were expecting us to arrive that evening and we were early. The market was in full swing and people were busy with their daily business. They didn't tell us to come back later – in half an hour's time, the market was closed and there were 200 people in the meeting house. Imagine sitting for 3 hours in the heat and 100 per cent humidity with no air conditioner and no complaints. Those people may lack our modern conveniences and material things, but the love of Christ in their hearts knows no bounds! (Matthew 6:33)

Everywhere we went we saw people eager to hear God's word. People who had so little gave so much and their Christian love spilled over in their laughter and happy smiles and blessed us again and again. It made me feel I was seeing a sample of Paul's New Testament Churches.

There were so many things I could write about. I got embarrassed at one place when they passed a bowl around to wash in and I was the first one to get it. I washed both hands. Everybody else just washed their right hand. (A custom peculiar to Moslems and their culture).

When someone came to a meeting late, he didn't slip quietly into a back seat; he came and shook hands with the speakers and a number of the audience before he sat down.

There were dogs and chickens walking freely among us while we spoke, and cats playing in the thatched roofs, (probably chasing rats and birds up there). I had looked forward to hearing Christopher speak but when he did he was translating, and I couldn't understand him.

Our meetings were not regimented with any set form. We just followed the Spirit's leading and watched God work in their midst with their lives and ours. The people were so open and at ease and loving that it cheered my heart just to see them.

It was a marvelous time for me and I shall continue to pray for those Christians and praise God for giving me the chance to go!

We had 28 meetings in 2 weeks and there were 25 Baptism's and 6 house visits. We also got home 5 hours late!

When John got home, he was so excited about what God had allowed him to do he could hardly contain himself.

NORMA WIGGINS
My Mom And Missions

On May 1, 1926, James O. and Mallie Wiggins welcomed the sixth member of the family, a baby girl, Norma May. This non-headlined event occurred in the small oil town of Hull, Texas, near Beaumont. Shortly thereafter, the family moved to Beaumont, and with a baby boy, completed their family of seven, four boys and three girls. I tell you this to let you know that this was occurring during the Great Depression, and times were difficult.

We may not have had material wealth, but we had a great wealth of family love and faith in a heavenly Father, who was always near. I remember that my Mom made sure we were in Sunday School and church on a regular basis, whether or not she was physically able to go with us. It was a way of life for us.

It was through Mama that I first heard of WMU. It was a time when the "circles" of this great organization met in individual homes, had an informational program about the mission field, gave a mission offering, prayed for the missionaries and made plans for the future.

I don't know when I first heard the story of Lottie Moon, but I was young. Her life and sacrifice were an ideal that inspired me greatly.

As a small church, we did not have such groups as Sunbeams, GA's and Acteens, but through the years I learned the story of missions, particularly foreign missionaries. I had no idea that one day I would actually meet some of them face-to-face, but I have and it is a privilege on each and every occasion.

After retirement, I have been able to participate in our local Women on Mission organization by finding musicians who share their talents for our monthly luncheon and meeting. We also have a night group who meet once a month to learn about current mission trips.

I have not physically "gone on the field," but through prayer and as much financial help as possible, I feel that I am participating in the Great Commission to tell the world about salvation through Jesus. In the words of the hymn, "The longer I serve Him, the sweeter He grows."

Join us, won't you?

Norma Wiggins, Austin TX -- 9/15/13

Joan Moore

My husband and I made two mission trips to the east coast of the United States.

Our trips were with a church choir we were associated with. We went to a small church in Maine and did Bible school while others worked on repair/construction for the pastor. We had the 5th grade department and we had about 8 students. One of our group accepted Christ! It was a wonderful experience working with the children and others in the church. We also sang in a park located within the town.

Our second trip was to New Jersey and New York. We represented a new, small church and very early each morning we (rain or shine) met the trains commuting into New York City. We handed out breakfast bars and a leaflet inviting the people to attend the church. We were also able to sing and love the people in one nursing home. We also did some prayer walking through a neighborhood in the town where we stayed. In addition, we also helped with some painting in the interior of a Baptist ministry office.

These trips were after 9/11/01. Some of the people were not too receptive; however, some were receptive and we pray we made a difference.

Doris Carlson Baker

I have been interested in missions since I was a young girl. I married my first husband, Earl Carlson, in 1952. We were both interested in missions. We had two sons who also grew to love missions. My younger son went on several trips into the interior of Mexico. My grandson, Benji Carlson, went to Peru on two mission trips. He was a UT student and member of the Hyde Park's F.O.C.U.S. group. My husband died in 1980.

I met Buck Baker in 1988 while volunteering on the line for Wednesday night dinner. We married in September 1988—my mission life was just beginning!

We went to Brazil, Australia, China, Japan, and twice to Russia.

Buck went home to glory in 1999. He told me if anything happened to him for me to "go do something good." I did—I went to Russia in November for 8 years with Buckner Orphan Care. We took shoes into the orphanages in the St. Petersburg area and loved on the kids and told them about Jesus. I've been blessed for the privilege.

"Go into all the world and preach the gospel...."

Virginia Kreimeyer's WMU Story

As a child, I was taken to Sunbeams on Wednesday evenings at the Baptist church in a small Mississippi town. I loved Sunbeams, learning songs, making crafts, and learning about missionaries in faraway places. My memories of being a Sunbeam were some of the happiest times. Later, when my family moved to Jackson, I joined Girls Auxiliary and participated in mission studies earning a Queen Regent title. One time I remember talking to the WMU Director, which was a big deal because she was a leader in the church, and she told me how she had always wanted to be a missionary but life had not turned out that way for her. So, she became the WMU Director to support missionaries around the world. I never forgot our conversation because I wanted to be a missionary, too.

God always has a plan for us and allows us to fulfill our dreams in ways we could not even imagine. For three years I served as WMU Director at Hyde Park and have served as a short-time missionary to Latvia, Mexico, and China as well as various sites in the U.S. What an amazing God we serve!

Virginia Kreimeyer and a friend

Dora Roberts

MY MISSION STORY TO DATE

"When I grow up, I want to be a WMU Lady!" This was my first heartfelt desire at age 4 as I accompanied my precious mother to a WMU meeting at our church, First Baptist of Hereford, Texas. I was number 12 of 13 children, and our mother was doing everything in her power to see to our Christian education. And it was effective. One of my older sisters, Florence and her husband Gerald Pinkston, served in Indonesia and South Africa a total of 40 years. Another older sister, Doris Parker, served as Minister of Music for East Grand Avenue Baptist Church in Dallas. Everyone else has been very active in churches all over the United States, so you can see I've had some awesome examples to follow.

My desire to serve God continued to grow as this little farm girl participated in Sunbeams and GA's until I reached Queen Regent. I moved to Houston with my mother and younger sister after our daddy passed away. I was still involved in church activities, but I did not feel God's call on my life for "special service" until I was 37 years old and an active member of Second Baptist Church, Houston. I was encouraged by Dr. Jim Deloach and Dr. Ed Young, my pastors, to get as much Bible training as I possibly could until the Lord gave me further instruction.

Then in 1980, I met John Ernest Roberts, and in July, 1981 we were married at Second Baptist Houston. At that time, I was on staff with the Billy Graham Crusade Office for the Gulf Coast Crusade of 1981. God is so good and especially when you put Him in first place in your life. This includes my dear son, David Wade Goldston, who worked as a driver for the Crusade Team and continues to walk closely with God.

Ernest had attended Southwestern Theological Seminary as a young man and longed to serve full time in the Lord's work. After moving to Austin and Hyde Park Baptist Church, and while teaching a large Sunday School Class of our peers, we began seeking where the Lord would use us. Then in 1993, we were assigned to mountain churches in Colorado. After NAMB sent us though training for this kind of work, we moved and served in churches in Salida, and in Estes Park Colorado for seven years.

In 1999, we were called to serve in East Tennessee for the next five years. We finally returned to Austin in 2006, due to the sad fact that my beloved husband was diagnosed with Alzheimer's. He lived only two more years. The Sunday before his last seizure we were in church at Hyde Park; he lived only two weeks before going to be with Jesus.

After recuperating for a few months, I was blessed to get back into work for my Lord and church. Among other joyful opportunities, I am blessed to serve as WMU DIRECTOR at Hyde Park this year, which I see as fulfilling my goal at the tender age of four years! I pray I can continue to be of service in the work of my Lord until I see Him face to face!

September 2013

This is the Instillation of Dora Roberts as WMU DIRECTOR. She was presented with several gifts, one being a Prayer Shawl from Jerusalem.

TIM JOLLY

In 1994, I joined the Austin Christian Bass Club for fun and recreation with other anglers who are Christians.

The requirements to join are to be a Christian and an active member of a local church. Every spring and fall we do things for the community. We take amputees out on the boats for a day of fishing. Another activity we do is take kids with disabilities out fishing, called "Cast for Kids." This is a national event during April through May that each Saturday there are about 8 events going on at the same time across the country.

Last, but not least, we take out the children from the Texas Baptist Children's Home in Round Rock for a day of fishing, fun and games at Gatti Land in Round Rock.

These events have one thing in common and that is—we share the love of Christ with people, and it gives us an opportunity to witness to them through the sport of fishing.

Linda Everton

In 2006, I sent 250 cubes with Kathy French and the Acteens that showed how to become a Christian. And I sent money with them to aid them in getting the cubes to Latvia with them. They also took shoes, socks, and clothing for the orphanage children. We had a drive at the church to get money and clothing for them to pack and ship. When our ladies left Latvia, they placed a cube on the desk of every teacher in the Riga schools they had worked with. It was a great irony that the teachers were allowed to use the cubes in class there and we could not in Austin.

From **Kathy French** to Linda Everton:
We used the money you gave us to take Evangecubes to Latvia. We used them in Riga at the Vilandes Baptist Church in Riga at the VBS we did there and also at the Piladzite Bernu Nams Orphanage (which is now a

home for disabled adults). It was a great time and the Evangecubes were a great help to our ministry! Several children and teenagers received Christ during that time. God is good!

Beth Everton

This letter was sent to multiple young people in the Chapel Choir after their trip to Toronto, Canada, Summer 0f 2013. This particular copy was presented by Beth Everton.

Dear TEXAS Friends.   June 18th 2013.

I wanted to let you all know that it was a pleasure meeting you. I love all of your personalitys, you guys are all very nice and fun to be with. I know that you guys aren't going to be around much long but after today I hope that you guys will come back at some point, but if not then its ok. I realy apreciate what you guys are doing for us. You are all realy a nice group of people, you're all respectfull, sociable and amusing to be with. I'm writting you guys this letter to thank you all for coming to joliette. Its fun for me to meet other people who speek english. I also wanted to say that I realy enjoyed the activities yesturday so thats why im here today, to support you all today. Keep it going and I hope that we can keep in contact.

PS: Sorry if i cant remember your names.
Love you all
   Laïla Landry

David Parker
Music Mission Trip to Sao Palo and Brasilia, Brazil
June 2010
Camp Kirkland's Global Mission Project

Music Foreign Missions, really?

In the days of my *tender and callow youth* (50's and 60's), foreign missions meant going to a primitive, third world country and living and ministering in the "outback" to the natives. This is still the case in many areas of the world, but trends in the last 30 years have changed this to a remarkable degree. Most "third world" countries, while still primitive in many ways, are notably modern in urban areas. Electronic technology has brought these areas into the 20th/21st Centuries. This means that they understand modern (Romantic/Jazz) music, and many appreciate the performance of contemporary Christian music.

About 20 years ago, a successful arranger/composer of contemporary Christian Music was persuaded that there was a possible mission project to the cities of the third world and that perhaps some American musicians would be interested in going on mission to these areas. Camp Kirkland explored this opportunity and was able to start the Global Mission Project. Since then, he has taken various music ensembles to many areas in Eastern Europe, South and Central America, the Caribbean Islands and South Africa.

The ensembles are in three categories:

A) What a studio musician calls a Tenor Band, (7-10 players, usually Saxophones, Trumpets, Trombones, Piano, Bass and Drums, maybe Guitar.)

B) A 1940 Big Jazz Band (Dorsey, Miller, Basie) 17-21 players.

C) A Studio Orchestra, a Big Band plus some additional Flutes, Oboes, Bassoons and French Horns, and 10-12 Strings. Most film scores are recorded by a similar ensemble. Camp expressed the desire some day to take a full symphony on a GMP mission; getting good string players is the problem.

Musicians from HPBC have been on several of the GMP missions:

-Tim Todd, our lead Trumpet, went to the Ukraine as lead trumpet in a Metro Big Band.

-Nick Farrell, former HPBC Orchestra Director, as Baritone Sax in a Metro Big Band went to Finland.

-John Broughton, Tenor Sax, as *ride* Sax in a Tenor Band to Austria/Hungary, as *ride* Sax in a Metro Big Band to Ukraine and to South Africa.

-David Parker, French Horn, went to Brazil in a Studio Orchestra.

Some similarities to all these Missions: Facilities are generally like anything in North America. Describing the hotels where we stayed in San Paulo and Brasilia to my son, a Hospitality Pro; they are 2-3 Diamond facilities and better than many Motel Sixes. Very comfortable, and the desk clerks understood more English than my minimal Portuguese. Breakfast was more than ample and very good. Lunch and Dinner was at local restaurants and also very good and not expensive, by Austin standards. Tim, Nick, and John confirmed this was their experience. No sleeping in thatched roof huts and cooking over an open fire.

My Mission was a little different, as we had a larger ensemble and did some Master Classes, in addition to playing concerts and Church services. In North America, we are used to Music being taught in the Public and Private Schools as part of the general curriculum. This is not the case in Brazil and much of Eastern Europe. The tradition in these areas is for the primary user of musicians to train them in their own facilities. In Brazil, this is the Roman Catholic Church where music is almost exclusively vocal, and not instrumental. Protestant Churches try to deal with this, but frequently don't have the facilities to do much more than the three R's. As a result, there are not many amateur musicians of sufficient quality to perform in church orchestras. There is an additional problem, in that there are no Instrument manufacturers or importers of woodwind or brass instruments, because there is not a significant elementary/secondary music program. Sounds like a "catch 22" to me. Musicians in Brazil had to acquire skills by private study and many had not had experience in ensemble performance. The Master classes were aimed at introducing the few church musicians to the literature available from American publishers and to some more advanced teaching techniques common in American secondary schools. High School bands and orchestras almost do not exist in Brazil. Maybe this is because soccer is their national sport rather than football.

Please NOTE: When teaching a technical subject thru an interpreter, speak slowly in 7-10 word sentences! Always!

Some of the churches we performed in had a few instrumentalists that eagerly joined us. This may have been the first opportunity they had to rehearse and perform with a full ensemble. In both cities a very good amateur Horn player showed up to play with us. Both Hornists were good enough so Kim and I (Kim was the other North American Hornist in the group) gave them the first part and let them play the solos. Try coaching someone that speaks only Portuguese. Fortunately, the universal language of Music (Italian) saved the day. Some of the churches had what seemed to be extensive string programs. A few questions revealed that while there are several very good Luthiers (string instrument builders), importing Woodwind and Brass instruments is almost impossible.

One church in San Paulo informed Camp that the choir had learned a vocal/orchestral piece that he had written several years before and wanted to perform it with us, and they had the orchestral parts. We virtually sight read the performance with Camp conducting, but the choir singing in Portuguese. A little understanding of Spanish and Italian made some sense of the vocal cues in our parts. The performance went quite well, considering that only a few of the players had significant orchestra performing experience. A few were near symphony class players but others were closer to early High School.

I noticed that Churches over 40 years old were complete and well maintained, but newer buildings seemed to be still under construction. The Brazilians explained that since the Catholic Church was entirely funded internally, or with assistance from the Vatican, the Brazilian Banks do not make loans to churches, especially Evangelical churches. As a result, construction is in stages and paid in cash. Some Evangelical churches were short on finish internally, but had good electronic systems; the influence of television evangelism from North America.

Some of our players were from Brazil but are living in North America. They were able, with some practice, to speak to the congregations in Portuguese and give testimonials about Music in the Church. One player was from San Paulo, but was finishing a Doctoral degree in Applied Flute at The University of North Texas. Gabriela spoke English with a North Texas accent and played Symphony class Flute. When we did instrument demonstrations at some of the schools, Camp expected us to play Hymn tunes, but when Gabby's turn came, she played the *Bird theme from Peter and the Wolf*. So I did the *Imperial March from Star Wars*. Camp was not amused! But the kids thought it was great. Later we kidded Gabby that all they teach for Flute at UNT are "birdcalls." (This is a reference to a MASH TV episode.)

Some cautions:

1) To keep costs down, expect an overnight flight both going and coming.

2) While credit cards are generally accepted, make your first stop in country at an ATM machine. Get some local currency!

3) Try to pick up some of the local language in advance. Thank you, Hello, Good-bye, God Bless, no habla Portuguese, etc. is always helpful and appreciated.

4) Costs: Most participants pay their own way.

Originally, Camp tried to keep costs in the $2500 to $2700 range, but prices are rising. We paid about $2900 plus $600 for food, etc., three years ago to go to Brazil. The trip to Hungary this July 2014, starts at $3200 plus. Closer locations will be less. Cuba has been averaging $1700. Yes, Camp can get you in and out of Cuba. Music Evangelism is very appreciated and the Cubans respond, a lot!

Is all this worth it? I say yes! The Brazilians were very helpful, and there seemed to be a significant response to invitations given after our performances. It is a little hard to gauge the effect of our Music, but the appreciation level was very high. While these trips are treated as Foreign Missions, you do get to do some touring. Brasilia, the most modern national Capital in the Americas, was very interesting, and we got to attend a rehearsal of the National Symphony and a performance by the San Paulo Symphony. As luck would have it, I missed the San Paulo concert because of the "Brazilian flu." I was really disappointed, as the program was *"Le Sacre du Printemps,"* which I last heard playing 8th Horn for three performances with the San Antonio Symphony.

To any Musicians thinking of going on a GMP Mission: The Music is similar to what most large churches perform in the Sunday morning services. Discussions with other musicians indicated that our parts from the Brazil trip were similar to what many of us had played that spring in our home churches. If you are comfortable with this, don't hesitate about the Music part of the Mission.

JOYCE PARKER

On November 19, 1949, my brother, Jimmy, and I both made our professions of faith on that Sunday morning and were both baptized that night. We went down into the water side-by-side at the same time! I remember that date because it was my Grandma Turner's birthday. I was nine years old and my brother was eight, so it was not a big heavy task for Bro. J. Travis Gibson to baptize us this way. Our church, FBC, New London, Texas, began a building program shortly afterward. I remember that our whole congregation was involved in this project, even us kids. Some of us younger ones were scraping the paint off the windowpanes to reuse in the new Sunday School rooms. And we took iced tea and Kool Aide to the men doing the real work. After we were having services in the new church, our Daddy was ordained as a deacon and began driving the church bus, bringing people from miles around to hear the word of God by way of Bro. Gibson. His two sons, Joe and David, would ride with Daddy sometimes. The parsonage was next to the church and the bus was parked nearby. Mother also sent us three Turner kids with Daddy so that she could have some time to herself. Joe would lead us all in singing all the "newest" choruses in the early 1950's.

We were a small church, and I do not remember having GA's, but we did go to Piney Woods Baptist Encampment where we heard missionaries speak. When I was sixteen, Daddy was transferred from New London to Luling, and there at Central Baptist Church I enrolled in YWA's. Then after graduation, I moved to Austin and joined Hyde Park Baptist Church in July, 1960, just a few months after Dr. Ralph M. Smith began his ministry there. One of my schoolmates at Brackenridge Hospital School Of Nursing, Sally Jo Bowmer, was a life-long member of HPBC and encouraged me to join. Here again, we had YWA's. They had a "White Bible Ceremony" for me a few days before I married David Edgar Parker, April 19, 1962.

Going back a few years, while in high school, I went to Alto Frio Camp in Leaky, TX with our music director and his wife who played the piano/organ. It was there that I surrendered for "special service," not really knowing what that might involve. With the help of a nurse friend of Mother's, I enrolled in Brackenridge Hospital School of Nursing in Austin, and began considering this an answer to my call to "special service." After graduation, I worked in several hospitals' operating rooms here in Austin in my forty-four year career. I prayed for my patients, held their hands as they were being anesthetized for surgery, and sometimes as they were waking up afterward. At one hospital, I started the intravenous drips, and since I used a drop of local anesthesia, some of them called me "Painless Parker!" So...I considered the alleviating of anxiety about surgery as my mission.

As soon as I retired in 2005, I attended the Mission Fair at Hyde Park and signed up to knit scarves for the Magdalene Project, (I knitted 100 scarves!) and across the room was "talked into" teaching knitting for Friendship International of Austin. Did you know that working in Friendship is like being a Foreign Missionary without leaving town? We average 25 countries represented in a semester! What an experience for this East Texas girl! After only two semesters, I was invited to be on staff as Coordinator of Classes. I had no clue what this would involve, since I was told, "there's nothing to it." Yeah, there is! Making sure there are teachers for the 20 some-odd classes is a big deal! But what a blessing it has been to become friends with ladies from all over the world, and to let them know of Jesus' love for them! This is my eighth year serving in Friendship.

About four years ago, (2011), I decided to go to the WMU First Tuesday Mission Luncheon---a few weeks before the election of officers. I was asked to be the Coordinator of WOM. I said, "I don't even know what that is! How can I coordinate it?" The explanation is: WMU is the umbrella over WOM, ACTEEN's, GA's, RA's, and MISSION FRIENDS. "But what does WOM stand for?" Women On Mission, duh. "How can I do this, since I've never even been in WMU before?" I was told to read about Moses and Gideon, because they had never done anything either. So, here I am still coordinating WOM!

This is the 125th Anniversary of the national WMU. The motto this year is THE STORY LIVES ON. I read a book by Wanda S. Lee, Executive Director, National WMU. The book has the same title, and I heard a voice in my head "You can do that!" Hers was a collection of WMU mission stories, so I began collecting Hyde Park mission stories to compile into a book, HYDE PARK'S MISSION STORY LIVES ON. Hopefully, it will be one that our church body can be proud to read, give, and own, because our story will live on until Jesus Christ returns.

HYDE PARK MISSION TRIPS PLANNED FOR 2014

Student Ministry
Guatemala
March 9-15

College/Singles Ministry
Boston, MA
March 9-15

Hispanic Ministry
Marble Falls, TX
April 17-19

International Ministry
Beijing, Fujian & Kinmen
April 29-May 12

Family Ministry
Highland Lakes Camp
May 2-4

International Ministry
South Sudan
May 27-June 7

Acteens Ministry
Worcester, MA
June 28-July 5

&

Romania
July 27-August 4

WMU MISSION TRIPS

Salt Lake City, Utah
June 24–28, 2014
FamilyFest

Eastern Kentucky
July 19–24, 2014
FamilyFest

Toledo, Ohio
October 1-5, 2014
MissionsFest

Printed in the United States
By Bookmasters